C0-AJQ-618

12.00

Practical Business Models

OTHER BOOKS BY THE SAME AUTHORS

*Analysis Bar Charting – a simplified
   critical path analysis technique* J. E. Mulvaney
                                      (Mantec Publications)

*The Use of Network Analysis in
   Marketing*   J. E. Mulvaney
                                      (Institute of Marketing)

Market Models   C. W. Mann
                                      (Mantec Publications)

-Practical Business Models-

J. E. MULVANEY

C.Eng., M.I.E.E., M.I.M.C.

Director, The Whitehead Consulting Group Ltd

C. W. MANN

M.Sc., C.Eng., M.I.Mech.E., M.I.M.C., A.M.B.I.M.

Director, Lockyer Whitehead Ltd

A HALSTED PRESS BOOK

JOHN WILEY & SONS New York

163102

658.4
M 9611

Published in the U.S.A. by Halsted Press, a Division of
John Wiley & Sons, Inc. New York.

© J. E. Mulvaney and C. W. Mann 1976
First published 1976

Library of Congress Cataloging in Publication Data

Mulvaney, John Edward.
    Practical business models.

    "A Halsted Press book."
    1. Industrial management—Mathematical models.
2. Models and modelmaking. I. Mann, Clive W., joint author. II. Title.
HD38.M83   658.4'034   75-33219
ISBN   0   470-62386-1

Printed in Northern Ireland at The Universities Press (Belfast) Ltd.

Preface

This is not an academic book. The reader will find no extensive bibliography, no long list of references to the work of other authors, and very little mathematics. It is a book written for managers, not for specialists in model-building. It is based upon the work carried out since the mid-1960s by consultants of the Whitehead Consulting Group Ltd, in cooperation with their clients.

The book deals with the pioneering days of business models in the U.K. and Europe. It is concerned with what has been done, with what has been found to be of lasting value, and with what is now practical. It explores model-building without using the jargon, or indeed the legitimate technical language, that characterizes some texts on the subject. Models for use by managers should be capable of explanation using normal management terms.

We are too close to the work we review, both in terms of time and involvement, to be able to claim to be making an objective assessment of the period, but we hope that someone will do this later on. What we have done is to report to our readers some of the developments in the use of models by managers, by means of a series of cases, based on the work that has been carried out. Our approach is therefore entirely practical. At the same time, some ten years' experience has helped us to develop a certain number of principles which now underlie this type of work.

These principles are dealt with in the first two chapters, and in the final chapter. The remaining chapters deal with applications. In all but one case, the companies have been disguised.

It is our hope that managers who read the book will get from it a deeper understanding of the nature and power of models. More important, we hope that they will be able to relate their own pressing problems to those described in the cases, and that the way to possible solutions may be indicated.

JOHN MULVANEY
CLIVE MANN

Contents

1. *Everyone Uses Models*

Man's first attempt at building a model possibly occurred when a primitive man drew a representation of an animal on the wall of his cave. Cave drawings might even have been the first business models. 'Good morning, gentlemen. We are in the business of killing animals for food. Look at model A here. If you see that type of animal, run away. Now look at model B. This is not so dangerous, and is good to eat. So if you see one of these, insert your spear at the point marked with an X on the model.'

It seems that man has used models for almost as long as he has existed. Very early on he started producing representations of reality, or what he thought was reality, or tangible representations of his imaginings and fantasies. The key word is 'representation'. 'Model', as the word is used in this book, means something that represents something else. This is a very broad definition (including, for instance, some Members of Parliament), and we shall have to use a series of adjectives to qualify the word. We have already, in the title of the book, used 'practical' and 'business', by which we mean models that can be used effectively by managers to help with running a business.

CLASSES OF MODEL

Numerous examples of models in use come to mind readily. A model of a new car, built in clay; a model of yet another proposed design for rebuilding Piccadilly Circus, constructed in cardboard and plaster; or the mock-up of Concorde at Orly Airport. A model that physically resembles the real thing that it is intended to represent can be called an iconic model (Greek: *eikōn*, an image).

Another class of model in widespread use is described by the adjective 'analogue'. In this class one quantity is used to represent another: a simple example is a graph, where distances on a piece of paper are used to represent, say, time and sales volume. Another example is a depot-location model, constructed of weights, string and pulleys. The weights represent demands on the depot from different customers, and the point at which the joining knot comes to rest is the ideal theoretical place to put the depot.

The third general category of models, and the one dealt with almost exclusively in this book, may be called symbolic models. In this category symbols are used to represent quantities and the relationships between them.

A wide range of symbols exists, such as

$$ 1 \quad 2 \quad 3 \quad 4 \Sigma \int \sigma \sqrt{} \quad \$ \, £ > \nleqslant = \times \div \pi \, n \, P \, x^n $$

as does a whole series of rules for manipulating these symbols – rules of accounting, arithmetic, calculus, statistics, econometrics, commonsense, etc. In short, a set of powerful tools is available for analysis and synthesis in business.

Like the iconic and analogue models we have mentioned, symbolic models have been in use for many years. Noah's logistic support system for the Ark, for instance, was probably based on a symbolic model:

Volume of hay required (assume 200-day voyage)
2 elephants @ 0·1 cubic cubits per day × 200 = 20
2 giraffes @ 0·05 cubic cubits per day × 200 = 10
etc.
Total volume 286
Safety stock (5 percent) 14·3
$$ \overline{300{\cdot}3 \simeq 300} $$

Simulations like this no doubt helped him to decide the layout of the Ark.

A real example of a symbolic model is Leonardo da Vinci's calculation of the number of men required to shift a quantity of earth, often to be found framed in work study experts' offices, to show how long their trade has been established, and to add a little cultural flavour.

Business men have always used symbolic models. Bob Cratchit sitting on his stool wielding his quill pen was probably building a model of Scrooge's business, using the language of double-entry book-keeping. Accountants are the longest established model-builders in business, although their traditional tools and language suffer from some limitations, and need to be supplemented if they are to be used to build really good business models.

Man has a long experience of building explicit models using symbols. Scientists and engineers lead in this area. The model $f_0 = 1/2\pi\sqrt{LC}$ (resonant frequency calculation) was probably used when your television set was designed. Moving away from 'exactness', and somewhat in the direction of business,

$$t_e = \frac{a + 4m + b}{6}$$

enables a project manager to estimate the probable duration of an activity on his PERT network ('t_e' is the time used for planning, 'a' is the optimistic time, 'b' is the pessimistic time and 'm' is the most likely time for the activity).

INTANGIBLE MODELS

All the models mentioned so far are tangible. They are drawn on paper, or constructed of some material, and can be seen and touched. But there is an entirely different class of model, which no one can see and no one can touch. These are the intangible models, and the ones of interest are inside managers' heads, stored in some undefined way somewhere in the hundred million neurons in their brains. The models are there because the manager needs them to do his job. They got there by a process that starts with observation and entails many cycles of thought, by an evaluation and storing of the experiences the manager has in his present job, and in other jobs he has done, from books he has read, courses he has attended and so on.

Usually, the models are verbal – the manager uses words to describe them. Not very often are they mathematical. The following conversation illustrates the point.

'Please describe the market for your product.'
'Ah, yes, well, it's quite a complex set-up really. It's growing like mad in money terms and also in volume terms, but not as fast. There's us and there's Heinz and we seem to have about equal shares now. The others are not important, except the 'own label'

bit, but I think that's flattening off now, although I'm not sure about Marks and Sparks. I think the last Nielsen shows 'others' as ten per cent – it was fifteen per cent when I took over from Jim.

'Then there's the changes in distribution patterns – we are losing out in chemists, in share terms I mean, but our new variety range should correct that . . . etc.'

If the manager is good at his job, his verbal model will be a good representation of his market. Based on it, he can give a good description of the market structure and dynamics, and may be able to predict its behaviour in future. He will know what is important and what is not. He will have a feel for the likely moves of his competitors. He has played the game many times before, and knows the rules. Similar responses can be obtained by asking a financial controller about the effects of seasonality on cash flows, or a production controller about the effect of machine reliability on inventory levels.

These verbal models are far from exact, but they are good enough to manage with, at least in the manager's judgement No one builds exact models of anything. A man may know that his wife has a mole on her tummy, but he does not know that its centre is 2·8645 in. from the centre of her navel.

EXPLICIT MODELS

Of course, managers often have a great deal of data with which they can extend and quantify their verbal models when they need to. For example:

'You said your market was growing like mad. Can we look at the figures?'

'Yes. Here is a graph showing volume growth in moving-annual-total terms over the last fifteen periods. We have corrected for Nielsen's under-reporting. The correction factors are shown in the Appendix, and how we got them. You'll see they changed in period twelve . . . etc. etc.'

Here the manager is using an explicit model, built with symbols and displayed as a graph. In most management jobs it is necessary to build models such as these, and to use them in conjunction with verbal models.

ALL MANAGERS USE MODELS NOW

Figure 1.1 shows how managers use models. It represents the total interaction between a company and its market and resources environments. The bottoms of the triangles represent the 'real' interactions that take place – the many millions of individual activities such as those shown.

Very few people manage by observing these real interactions, however. They use models. For instance, a brand manager uses a chart showing movement in percentage share of the market, the buyer economic batch quantity tables, and the managing director cash flow calculations. Even when managers are directly concerned with real interactions, they use models. The foreman in the milling shop has his rack of job cards, the vehicle scheduler has his routing charts, and the desk clerk allocating a hotel bedroom, which he has probably never seen, puts the visitor into a hole in his booking matrix.

Managers in business organizations have so far been described as equipped with the verbal models they have in their heads, and having access to a number of explicit models that they have built themselves or have had built for them. These explicit models have grown out of the job are usually simple, and are designed to help in the manager's decision-making processes.

Such were the starting conditions for all the model-building examples in this book. In all cases the work boils down to an extension of existing models, using rather more powerful tools than have been used before. Before looking at these examples, it is best to consider model-building in general, paying particular attention to the interaction between the manager and the model-builder.

THE PROCESS OF MODEL-BUILDING

Both the manager and the model-builder have parts to play in the process of model-building. They are referred to in the singular, although, in larger applications, teams of managers and model-builders are concerned. Their interaction is both close and complex. The model-builder cannot build a model *for* the manager, he can only build it *with* him. The manager cannot build a model without

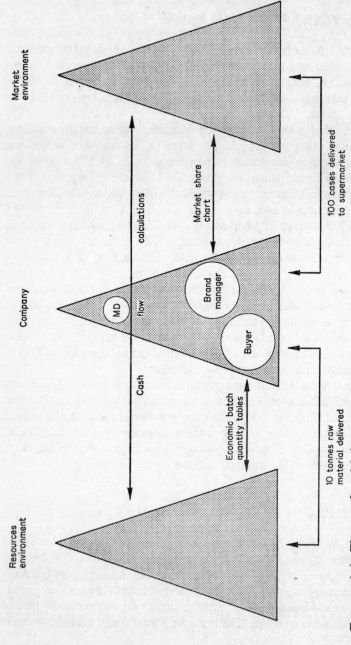

FIGURE 1.1. The use of models in a company.

the model-builder, simply because he does not have the time, nor often the necessary technical skills.

The process applies to any model-building project, be it the design of a system for investment planning across Europe, the production of a population-forecasting model, or a model to predict the response to a particular marketing plan. A number of stages can be identified. These are not presented as a standard procedure that has to be followed for any model-building project. Rather, they are areas of work which require attention, usually following broadly the sequence shown.

However, the process of model-building often involves returning to earlier stages as a result of work carried out in the later ones. For this reason, the examples in the later chapters are dealt with in a way which concentrates on particular aspects of model-building rather than in the sequence shown below, though the following steps are always necessary at some time in a model-building project:

1 Selection of an area for application
2 Analysis and recording of management objectives, tasks and processes
3 Specification of management requirements
4 Definition of the logic of the model
5 Putting the model on a computer
6 Implementation – bringing the model into use
7 Maintenance and development.

SELECTION OF AN AREA FOR APPLICATION

This subject is covered in detail in Chapter 2, so at present it may just be noted that there must be a close interaction here between manager and model-builder. The manager knows about his operations and the model-builder knows what models can do. Together they can identify where models could be built, and then where they should be built.

ANALYSIS AND RECORDING OF MANAGEMENT OBJECTIVES, TASKS AND PROCESSES

Again Chapter 2 examines this aspect. It is of vital importance to get this stage right. If a man is going to use a model to help him make his decisions, it must be based on his present methods of operating. People will not readily make fundamental changes in the way they behave. At the end of this stage the managers should say, 'Yes, that's the way we really operate now. That is how we analyse and attempt to manipulate our situation.' (They may say also that it's the first time they have seen it down on paper. It is remarkable how many reasonably efficient processes have never been defined.)

SPECIFICATION OF MANAGEMENT REQUIREMENTS

This is a matter of specifying the improvements required to existing processes, or additions to be made. For example, 'In our five-year planning, we only have time to look at about two or three alternative plans. If management inject a fresh lot of assumptions half-way through the year, as happened last year, we have to work all night and at week-ends to work out the consequences. If it happens again this year I'm likely to end up divorced!' And again, 'It's all very well running out sets of figures based on market and sales forecasts. Now that we've got the financial model, this takes only half a day. What we really need is more reliable forecasts, or at least a sensible method of handling the uncertainty in them.'

From opening statements like this, gathered from *all* the managers concerned, a detailed specification can be drawn up to define the purpose of the model and its scope. Throughout this stage the focus is the job that the management has to do. The requirements grow out of the job, requirements for ways to relate key factors in a decision-making situation, requirements for information to support judgement. If a manager is simply asked what information he would like, he will produce a very long list that is of little use unless it is related to the logic of the management process.

This step itself sometimes produces valuable side-effects. In the construction of one model to forecast total demand in a market it was found that some vital data was not being obtained, and a great deal of money was being spent on market research data that was no longer relevant.

DEFINITION OF THE LOGIC OF THE MODEL

Having defined the logic of the management process, the way data is currently converted to information to support the processes, and what improvements and extensions everyone would like to see, the logic of the model can be defined. This is the set of rules that governs the activities within the model between the input and output. The quality of the model and its value to the user depend on this stage. This is the main creative element of the model-builder's task; the effective use of his insight and imagination at this point in the design process is essential. In addition, consideration is given to whichever part of the model, if any, could and should be run on a computer. This leads to the next stage.

PUTTING THE MODEL ON A COMPUTER

The computing facilities necessary, and the computer language to use, depend on the amount of data to be handled, the complexity of the calculations, the speed of response necessary, and the nature of the manager-model interaction. Computers generally appear twice in the process. Firstly, they are used during the model-building phase, when the logic of the model is being set up. The many statistical packages available on commercial time-sharing services are often employed by model-builders, when they are looking for relationships between important factors – for example, when trying to establish the seasonal pattern of invoicing, or the relationship between sales volume and discount levels.

Secondly, the management requirement may dictate that the model is used on a computer, either on a terminal to which the manager has direct access, or via a computer department or bureau.

IMPLEMENTATION – BRINGING THE MODEL INTO USE

If the process of model-building has been performed correctly, the managers concerned will be eager to try *their* model. (They will not regard it as the model-builders' model.) The model-builder may be required to provide assistance with the mechanics of the computer for an initial period, and will also be available to remind the managers about the logic of the model and the assumptions built into it.

MAINTENANCE AND DEVELOPMENT

Like any other piece of machinery, a model-based system requires maintenance, and may need modification over a period of time.

Models represent reality, and reality changes. Models must keep in step.

A TEAM APPROACH

As a model-building project develops through the stages listed above, the people involved should become a closely knit team. Many skills have to be integrated, and much work has to be done, before the manager can sit down at a terminal and find his way to a good solution to a particular problem using his model. In fact, many things have to be done before the first key on a computer terminal is pressed. The next chapter deals with some of these.

2. *Where and How*

In the first chapter we said that the initial step in the use of models was to select an area for application. In this chapter we discuss a procedure for identifying situations where models might be used, and suggest criteria for selection.

PLANNING AND CONTROL

Models are being used effectively in planning, deciding what to do, and how to do it. The model-builder, as we have so far called him, must understand the logic of planning and be a competent planning-system designer. Models are also being used in the control function; monitoring results and comparing these with plans. Our model-builder, therefore, needs to be something of a cybernetician!

When looking for possible application areas, it is these two aspects – planning and control – which repay the effort of analysis.

DIVERSITY IN PLANNING REQUIREMENTS

The type and extent of planning that an organization needs depends clearly upon its size and the type of commercial or industrial activity in which it is engaged. At one end of the scale stand large international organizations, with diverse operations in many countries, and at the other end small firms with simple local operations.

In addition to these differences in scale, companies vary considerably in their management methods and styles, from the highly centralized authoritarian organization, where most important decisions are made by a small group of men at the centre, to those where the management style encourages a diffusion of decision-making throughout the structure.

It is, therefore, unrealistic to suppose that any single formalized planning system will produce results that are satisfactory in all cases. Planning systems can be designed only to suit particular organizations, and these systems must be based on the real needs of the particular managers who run them. This is not to say that no changes in management methods and styles are to be considered. In many cases significant improvements are possible. The point is that, in general, planning systems must satisfy the needs of managers, who should not be expected to satisfy the needs of planning systems. In a particular organization the planning system designer, therefore, must take the present situation as one starting point. He needs to be sensitive to this situation and to recognize the many subtle relationships that exist.

Despite this diversity of planning needs, experience has shown that there is a basic logic underlying all planning processes. This can be used as a starting point by planning system designers, from which an analysis of planning needs can be carried out. The objective is to determine those areas where model-based systems might be useful.

THE LOGIC OF PLANNING PROCESSES

All managers are familiar with the need to plan operations, to make decisions. There is nothing new in the concept, for planning has existed ever since man first achieved the ability to conceive objectives: In essence, planning involves finding the answers to two questions.

What do we want to do?
How best can we do it?

The questions are very simple, but the process of finding the answers can be complex, particularly in the case of large organizations.

This is not the place to attempt a summary of the extensive literature on planning, if indeed such a summary is possible. Instead, as an example, consider the simple representation of the basic logic of the corporate planning process as shown in Figure 2.1.

The diagram will be familiar. The classic corporate planning process involves the tasks of setting objectives, establishing the present position, predicting where the organization will be if existing plans are achieved, and analysing the environment and predicting changes in it. With this information, management can create planning options, evaluate them and select one or more for implementation: that process, in turn, provides the base for detailed

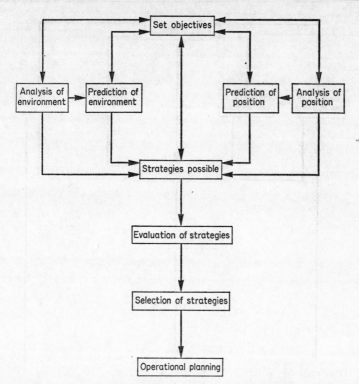

FIGURE 2.1. The logic of the corporate planning process.

planning of operations. A simple framework such as this can also be used to provide the basis for a complete analysis of the planning process currently in use.

THE LOGIC OF THE CONTROL PROCESS

Planning cannot be considered in isolation. Since all organizations operate in an increasingly changing environment, the control processes must also be considered. For example, plans need to be updated at appropriate intervals, either because of unpredicted changes in the environment, or because of variances between performance and plan.

Consider Figure 2.2, which represents the logic of both the corporate planning and control processes. The performance resulting

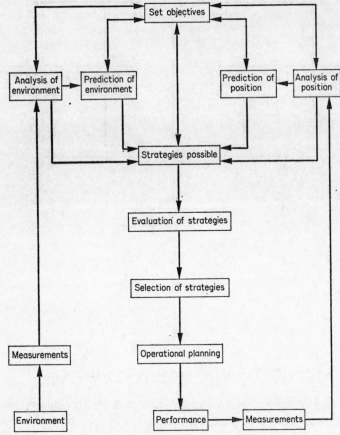

FIGURE 2.2. The basic corporate planning and control logic.

from operational planning must be measured, so that the position analysis and prediction can be updated. The environment too, must be measured, so that the environmental analysis and prediction can be updated.

CYCLES OF PLANNING AND CONTROL

Having used such a logical framework to analyse the planning and control processes, suitably modified and extended to suit particular organizations, the planning designer can then set these processes against a time scale, to produce a picture of the time cycles involved. Usually there will be an annual basis to these cycles.

A PERT representation of the cycles is often useful. Even at this early stage it is not unusual to find that the time available to carry out the various planning processes as well as managers would like, is insufficient. This gives an indication of where model-based systems might be used to speed up the necessary calculations or to allow management to look at more alternatives in greater depth.

SYSTEM PLANNING

The model-builder has, at this stage, produced his own 'model' of what management does, how it gets its ideas, and how it makes its decisions. It is important to ensure that this model is based on what really happens, and not on what managers say happens, or even on what they think happens. Sometimes managers are so involved in the actual production of plans that they lose sight of what has to be planned. It is not unusual to have to carry out a reorientation, to focus attention on to process and away from task.

The task of designing and installing planning and control systems may be termed system planning. The type of question that system planning must answer is indicated below:

How are objectives to be set?
How are objectives to be communicated?
What form should the analysis of the environment take?
What quantities should be measured, and how often?
What forecasting mechanisms should be used?
How should the environment be monitored?
How is the creation of strategies to be stimulated?
How are strategies to be evaluated; against what set of criteria should they be selected?
How is operational planning to be carried out?
What operational planning areas have to be considered and how are they to be coordinated?
What measurements of performance are necessary and how often should these be made?

All these questions, and the many others that arise, are concerned with the processes of planning and control, and not with the content of the plans. They are concerned with the methods used to create the plans – with the creation of the machinery of management.

Like other forms of planning, system planning needs to have associated controls. The functions of controls are to monitor the effectiveness of the machinery of management, and to modify and adapt it as management's needs change, so keeping it running smoothly.

PLANNING NEEDS

There are thus two types of planning necessary in an organization, as shown in Figure 2.3. Firstly, there is the planning of operations, which is concerned with both strategy and tactics. This type of planning should be carried out by managers with responsibility for operations – men with a strong task-orientation, who are anxious to answer the question 'What shall we do with our business?' and who are motivated to achieve good operational results. These are the men who tend to be strong leaders.

Secondly, there is system planning, which is dedicated to the production of systems of planning and control for the use of operational management. Managers concerned with system planning must have a strong process-orientation. They must be capable of taking a broad view of systems and must be sensitive to the real needs of operating management. They must understand what is desirable and possible in system terms. They must have a wide experience of planning and control techniques and must know how these can be applied effectively. Certainly they must understand and have experience in the use of model-based systems in planning and control. The man we have labelled 'model-builder' must have much more character and ability than that designation implies.

In the cases that are described in later chapters the model-builders were all consultants, and in some chapters appear specifically as such, though they can, of course, be members of an organization's staff. Internal or external, however, they must have a system-planning orientation if they are to succeed.

One footnote must be added to the above. Task-orientated managers are best suited for the planning and control of operations and process-orientated managers best suited to system planning; and by conscious or unconscious selection, the appropriate type of

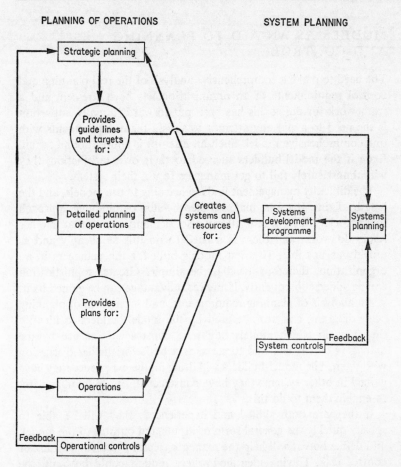

PLANNING OF OPERATIONS   SYSTEM PLANNING

- Strategic planning
- Provides guide lines and targets for:
- Detailed planning of operations
- Creates systems and resources for:
- Systems development programme
- Systems planning
- Provides plans for:
- System controls — Feedback
- Operations
- Operational controls — Feedback

FIGURE 2.3. Relationship between types of planning.

manager tends to occupy his relevant position in an organization. However, there is one important exception that must be made. The chief system-planner, while being fully aware of process, should also be strongly task-orientated. His task is to plan and install systems to provide operating management with effective processes. He should do this quickly and efficiently, and at the same time be a good team leader. The fact that such men are rarely to be found in this role probably explains why systems planning is often inefficient, and is not given the attention it deserves.

MODELS AS AN AID TO PLANNING AND CONTROL

The need to make a comprehensive analysis of the real planning and control requirements of an organization has been stressed, and a framework for doing this has been put forward. Equally important is the need to avoid any attempt to satisfy these requirements with one comprehensive model. Such an attempt is almost bound to fail. Even if the model-builders succeed to their own satisfaction, they will almost surely fail to get managers to use their system.

The difficulty management finds in learning to use models, and the length of time it takes, makes a step-by-step or modular approach mandatory. Most organizations also demand proof that models really do work, and there is a need to do this as cheaply and as quickly as possible. The first models built for the managers in an organization, therefore, need to be simple. Greater sophistication can be added subsequently, if any real advantage can be gained by it.

An analysis of planning requirements, and some form of planning cycle diagram, can now be used by the model-builders to identify the areas in which models might be constructed for use by the managers concerned, and to serve as a basis for further discussion with them. The model-builders will draw on the experience they have gained in other systems they have constructed, or are familiar with, to enable them to do this.

If they are both skilled and experienced, they will be able to specify quickly the general form of inputs and outputs of the model, and define how it will help the manager to carry out his planning or control task. Having identified where models could be built, the modellers must recommend where they should be built, and in what order. In other words, a system-development programme is prepared on the basis of the real priorities of the organization. Some of the factors that help to determine these priorities are discussed later.

SOME MODELS

MODELS DEALING WITH THE ENVIRONMENT

These examples are often concerned with markets. Management usually needs to have mechanisms that predict the size of markets over time periods ranging from one year to ten years. These models handle factors such as historical volumes, pricing effects, population trends, market-sector trends and movements between them, import and export volumes, possible technological developments, manufacturers' behaviour, macro-economic factors, and company assumptions regarding unpredictable items such as tax changes and actions of competitors. Purchasing models have also been constructed to handle factors such as alternative sources of supply and price movements. In most cases, however, management concern in the environmental area is directed mainly to its markets.

MODELS DEALING WITH POSITION ANALYSIS AND PREDICTION

The starting point here often turns out to be a series of models covering the organization's major products. One need is to have mechanisms that will help the managers in charge of the products to allocate marketing expenditure. Product models deal with factors such as the effect on market shares, or product volumes, of advertising, pricing policies, distribution, seasonal patterns, sales force activities, discounts and trade incentives, dealing and promotions.

The model-builder's task is to identify, with the manager, those factors that have a significant effect on product performance and to try to express those effects as 'influence functions', which are then incorporated in the model equations. Another need satisfied by product models is the forecasting of income or profit streams. Those forecasts are an essential input to the corporate planning function. Product models, therefore, usually take the calculations through to profit figures, and incorporate the relevant price and cost factors.

NEW-PRODUCT ACTIVITY

Many companies treat new-product activity as a separate planning and control area. Some model-based systems deal with the marketing and financial aspects of new products, and also handle the timing aspects, usually in the form of a simple PERT sub-system. Using such systems, managers can provide themselves with the latest data on any new product, or on the effects of total new-product activity on corporate performance.

FINANCIAL MODELS

The construction of financial models presents a somewhat different challenge from the construction of models of markets and products. They can usually be built more quickly, since less research and analysis are required to establish the financial and accounting relationship they contain, although these can sometimes be very complex. Financial models of products have already been mentioned. Other financial models provide investment analysis, cash flow, balance sheets, profit and loss statements, in fact all the commonly required accounting documents. These models, to be really useful to managers, must be constructed so that they are flexible, and they must enable a wide range of simulations to be carried out.

THE SYSTEM-DEVELOPMENT PROGRAMME

The system-development programme shows the various phases of development, with the earlier phases given in more detail. The time and cost for construction of each phase and results to be obtained are shown also. An example is given in Figure 2.4, which summarizes the system-development programme for a company in the tobacco industry. Several factors are important in deciding the sequence of development, but the more usual are the following:

PLANNING NEEDS

Sometimes it is possible to identify a really urgent need that the present planning method cannot satisfy. For example, in the case of a consumer goods company the time required for calculating the effects of pricing decisions and ingredient cost increases was far longer than the decision-time available. Consequently, the brand management were operating in an open-loop situation, with no ability to calculate the likely results of their decisions before the time came to make them. The construction of a model to solve the problem became Phase 1 of the system-development plan. In another case the first phase consisted of the construction of a financial model of the company, since the ability to simulate the outcome of alternative funding and investment decisions was urgently required.

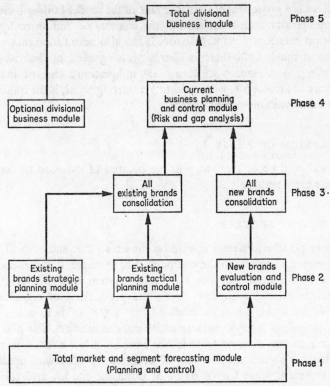

FIGURE 2.4. A typical system-development programme.

SKILLS AND ATTITUDES

When deciding where to start, the skills and attitudes of the managers for whom models might be built are sometimes important. If the model-builders are working with a manager who believes in the approach and himself has some degree of numeracy, they are more likely to succeed than if they are working with a hostile 'non-believer' with no numerate ability. Thus, in some cases, the major factor in selecting a starting point from several possibilities has been the keenness of the managers concerned.

DATA AVAILABILITY

The amount of data available, its reliability, and its structure are also important factors to consider when choosing a starting point.

If there is a great deal of data, the task of the model-builder increases in complexity and duration, but the chances of finding really significant relationships increase too. It has also been found that where there is much data there is also a pressing need to find ways of handling it – a means to cure 'data indigestion'. One of the key factors to investigate, when selecting a starting point, is the quality of the data available or obtainable.

DURATION OF PHASE 1

This should be as short as possible because of the need to demonstrate early results.

EFFECT OF SUCCESS

Where possible, Phase 1 should be chosen so that success will have a significant impact on the company. For example, the introduction of a model-based corporate planning system in one division of an international company led to the production of significantly better corporate plans, a much higher degree of innovation, and the analysis of many more alternative policies in depth. The planning cycle time was reduced from fifteen weeks to a few hours under this system. A significant increase of divisional profits was predicted by the management as a result of using the model, and this has subsequently been achieved. The success of the operation was very evident, and other divisions became interested in the approach.

The scene is now set for a closer look at particular cases, bearing in mind that the general considerations we have set out in these first two chapters form a backcloth to the cases described.

3. *Market Models*

This chapter deals with the construction and use of market models in a general way, as a prelude to the case-study treatment of particular markets in later chapters.

INTRODUCTION

Many companies' long-term prospects are geared closely to the prospects of their markets. This dependency, the need to understand more clearly the mechanisms at work in markets, and the need for better forecasting methods, have led to many attempts to build models that represent and predict market behaviour.

These attempts have been made more frequently in the markets for consumer products than in those for industrial goods. Examples of the use of models can be found in companies dealing in food, drink, tobacco, toiletries, cosmetics and pharmaceuticals. In the area of consumer durables examples can be found in the markets for products such as television sets, washing machines and motor vehicles.

In the U.K. and Europe, although consumer goods' companies led the way in the application of modelling methods, many models have now been constructed for industrial and commercial markets. Examples include models designed to predict demand for basic raw materials, for products such as pumps and valves for industrial services, and for other service industries such as hotel accommodation, insurance and shipping.

In this chapter the methods for building a model of a market will be outlined, by discussing and illustrating the processes in relation to markets for consumer goods. The problems are much the same as with markets for industrial goods, although the content is different. The illustrations are drawn from assignments undertaken over a number of years in a variety of consumer markets. The seven steps of the process are as described in Chapter 1 (p. 7).

SELECTION OF AN AREA FOR APPLICATION

There are many factors that could be considered before deciding on the selection of a market, including the following:

Present and possible future proportion of company sales it represents
Nature of competitive situation
Degree of stability
Degree of uncertainty
Degree of support and capability of managers concerned
Data availability and structure.

Typical examples arise in discussions of the starting point with managers, who make statements such as these:

'We must start with the baby food market because we are getting nowhere with increasing our brand share.'

'We don't need a model of the breakfast cereal market: it's as steady as a rock. We understand it completely.'

'We need a model of the breakfast cereal market because it's been steady as a rock for far too long. We need to upset that market, if we are going to get anywhere.'

'I just don't understand what's going on out there. Jim says the market research figures mean one thing, and Joe says they mean the opposite. We must get our ideas sorted out.'

'We have a pretty good forecasting method, which gives us total market volume projections, but we now need it broken down by sectors, and we need an updating mechanism for the consumption-by-age-group patterns.'

'If the industry is going to spend a quarter of a million on generic advertising, we'd damn well better get some idea of the kind of response we might get.'

This can be summarized by saying, 'Look for the sensitive areas'. Apply the treatment where success will remove the pain or improve the pleasure – thus selecting the market.

ANALYSIS OF OBJECTIVES, TASKS AND PROCESSES

The first step is to ask the manager concerned a number of questions. The start of a typical conversation is shown below:

Q. 'What are your overall objectives?'
A. 'I have to achieve the contribution targets which I agreed with my boss and he agreed with Zurich.'
Q. 'What major tasks do you carry out to get there?'
A. 'To begin with we make a marketing plan.'
Q. '*How* do you set about making the plan?'
A. 'Ah, that's a long story. We start from the forecasts of the size and value of the segments of the market.'
Q. 'Who produces these and what methods do they use?'
.... and so on.

The model-builder is analysing two things. The first is the existing models of the situation (the market), both implicit and explicit. The second is the management group's planning and control processes. He also analyses and records how these two aspects interact.

SPECIFICATION OF MANAGEMENT REQUIREMENTS

Once this process is complete he has enough information to state how a model of the market could be of use to the group. For example, the specification might begin as follows:

A total market model will be built with which the marketing group will produce forecasts for the total market consumption for the next ten years. These forecasts will be by segment of the market, by volume and value. Using the model, the group will be able to test the effect on demand of external events such as tax changes, price movements etc.

The specification would go on to deal with the model facilities in more, but not too much, detail. In practice the final system has

2

nearly always differed from the initial management specification, sometimes very much so. Models of this kind must be allowed to evolve during development. This is a natural phenomenon, except in the theoretical cases in which the management processes have been defined exactly from the outset.

DEFINITION OF THE LOGIC OF THE MODEL

With the end-use firmly in mind, the model-builder now gets down to a period of in-depth investigation, and intense creativity. He checks and cross-checks the manager's descriptive models against the explicit models that already exist in the form of charts, graphs, tables, etc. He checks the underlying data, and analyses it in as many ways as he thinks might be useful. During this examination the model-builder may make some discoveries, and confirm or deny certain assumptions. For example:

He may unearth an important factor that is unknown to the manager

He may unravel a trend that is at variance with the manager's ideas

He may confirm the manager's general ideas about the market, but be able to 'put the numbers on'

He may confirm in both qualitative and quantitive terms what the manager already believes

He may find no evidence in the figures to support the manager's ideas about a particular market mechanism

He will certainly find measurement errors in the data.

All these discoveries are useful, and will be discussed in depth with the manager as they arise. Either or both of the first will be enough to make the exercise worth while.

Creating the model logic will now be examined in more depth.

The model-builder's first step, in his task of assembling everything that is known about a particular market, is usually to determine what sources of data exist. In general there are three categories to examine – internal sources, market research reports and other external sources.

INTERNAL SOURCES OF DATA

The internal sources of data are those based on the company's own sales figures, generally split down by product type, pack size and possibly by product variety, and often sub-divided by geographical region or type of sales outlet. In many cases, particularly for food products, where the grocers are becoming increasingly dominated by large multiple chains, sales are broken down by major national accounts.

Whichever way the extracts of sales are compiled, it is important to examine them in detail in order to ascertain what they really mean. For example, it is quite possible for some of the product to go straight to the retailer, while a proportion is shipped to wholesalers for future distribution to retailers, and the resulting stockholdings in warehouses around the country have to be taken into consideration. By determining the pattern of distribution and stock levels, it is possible to relate the ex-factory sales to the amount actually available for sale by the retailer.

The model-builder, working in this way and discussing his ideas and conclusions with the manager, will examine all the relevant internal data in the hope that more light will be thrown upon the mechanisms operating in the market place. Reports from sales forces and discussions with salesmen are often very illuminating. For example, the following statement once led to an analysis of distribution performance that showed a company was ignoring its customers' prime need:

'They don't care very much about a short delivery period. It's reliability they want. They don't mind if it's three or four days, but when we say four, it's got to be four, not five or six.'

EXTERNAL SOURCES OF DATA

For consumer markets the model-builder will probably regard market research reports as his most important source of knowledge about the mechanisms at work. The data available varies with each market. The following types of report are available:

1 Retail audits of sales, through specified chains of shops, such as grocers, chemists, confectioners, tobacconists and newsagents. These audits cover sales to and from the retailer, both in volume and value terms, as well as giving an indication of price and product availability.
2 Consumer data, collected from a panel of housewives or other individuals, who record their purchases in a diary. The diaries

are collected by the market research company, and are analysed to show trends of consumer penetration and consumption rate. These diary panels are used both for fast-moving consumer products and for consumer durables. They are particularly important in markets where there is a multi-outlet pattern, and where any one measure of retail sales is unlikely to give the total picture of the market.

3 'Dustbin' panels, a variation on the consumer panel theme, where the housewife puts the empty product packages into a container and a researcher subsequently arrives to analyse and record her purchases. Obviously this can have certain advantages over relying on individual memories, but it imposes restrictions on the sort of products that can be measured.

4 In many companies there are 'one-off' market research reports, resulting from in-depth studies, often designed to measure consumer preferences for one product or another. In these reports there are often sufficient numbers included to give a 'snap-shot' of a market at a given point in time. These can be very useful for comparing one source of data with another.

5 For ethical pharmaceutical products, market research data is available from prescriptions written by a sample of doctors. This is collated both by product and by therapy.

Two other important sources of data are syndicates of manufacturers and government agencies. Syndicate data is sometimes available on markets where the manufacturers have an agreement to pool their sales figures, either by month or by quarter, or sometimes for the year, the total sales being collected by an independent body. These are then returned to the companies in the association. In this way each company has a good measure of the market.

Government data, particularly in the U.K., is very valuable. There are many statistics available in various ministries, and, in general, this data has been found to be reasonably accurate and, when interpreted correctly, to give reliable guides to trends in market and consumer demand. But, by their nature, these statistics are often not available in the degree of detail a company would like. The following are examples:

Central Statistical Office (U.K.): *Annual Abstract of Statistics*
Ministry of Agriculture, Fisheries and Food (U.K.): *Household Food Consumption and Expenditure.*

Office of Population Censuses and Surveys (U.K.): *Population Projections*

OECD: *Economic Outlooks*

Statistical handbooks on a country, particularly for East Europe, e.g. Hungary, Poland or the USSR.

REPRESENTING THE STRUCTURE OF THE MARKET

One important step in determining the logic of the model is to decide how to represent the structure of the market. A commonly used method is to consider a total market as being made up from several segments. This poses the problem of defining realistic segments. In some markets the traditionally accepted method of segmentation is not necessarily the one that is most useful to management. An example may clarify this point.

Structure of the U.K. cigar market. In the cigar market total sales are divided into segments that are defined by price ranges and physical size. There are four traditionally accepted main segments, but there has always been a strong demand for imported products. Sales of imported products are not included in the sales data compiled by the pool of British manufacturers, and such data was obtained from Customs and Excise sources, which published the figures monthly. When these figures were examined, imports were listed in terms of thousands of pounds weight by country of origin. The problem was to convert the weight figures into the number of units in each segment that this represented. By examining the main brands that were imported, and by using management experience on the type of cigars made in each country, conversion factors between weight and the size of cigars were derived.

When the model of the cigar market was constructed, in 1969, it was agreed that treating imports as a separate segment was misleading. The import volumes were therefore added to the four main market segments, which made sense as a model of consumer purchasing behaviour. A consumer has the choice of buying either a cigar manufactured in the U.K. or one manufactured abroad, and since consumer prices of imported cigars are very similar to those of home-produced ones, he is unlikely to regard imported cigars as a separate category. The numerical relationships were established by using other market research data, which was available in the company concerned with the investigation.

Once the imports had been added to the home-produced cigars, the sector trends were re-examined. It was found that some of the sectors were declining faster than expected, and another sector, which had appeared to be static, was in fact growing at a significant rate. Even at this early stage of work, management obtained significant new information from the data they already had, and were looking at their market in a new light.

Having more than one source of data on a market is a great asset, because it enables them to be checked against each other. However, the trends can be conflicting. A typical initial step is to draw graphs of say, the market volume trends from both sources, so that a 'picture' of their shape and magnitude can be examined.

A typical example is shown in Figure 3.1, where the data on the sales in a market measured by a consumer panel is compared with that from a retail audit. The panel data shows a decline in the market over the last eighteen-month period whereas the retail audit figures indicate that the market is comparatively stable.

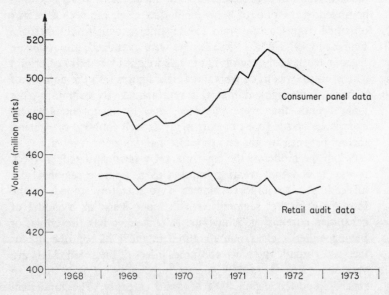

FIGURE 3.1. A consumer market – moving annual volume trends.

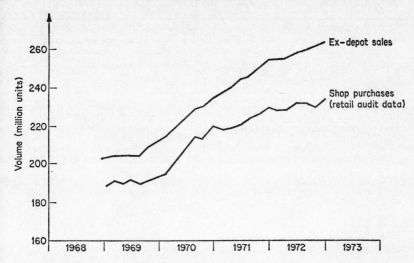

FIGURE 3.2. Comparison of volume trends from alternative sources for a consumer product.

In this case the apparent conflict was unravelled by comparing the sales of the company's own products with the sales recorded by the market research companies. This correction process was carried out by resolving the data on the market into its component trends, such as sales by type of outlet (e.g. multiple stores, individual shops and variety stores). The comparison enabled correction factors to be derived for each store type, and applied to the products in the market. A typical example is shown in Figure 3.2, where the market research data under-reports the actual sales by about 15 per cent. This figure also shows that the trend is changing with time.

It must not be assumed that the correction factors will remain constant. They must be monitored continuously for changes, which can be caused by many factors outside the company's control.

Once the correction factors have been calculated for each market segment, in this case by outlet type, the corrected volume trends can be put together to build up a picture of the true trend of demand in the market. This is illustrated in Figure 3.3, where the corrected market size is compared with the original trend reported by the retail audit data. The market was in fact growing slowly, with a size about 10 per cent greater than that recorded in 1968, and becoming 20 per cent greater by 1972.

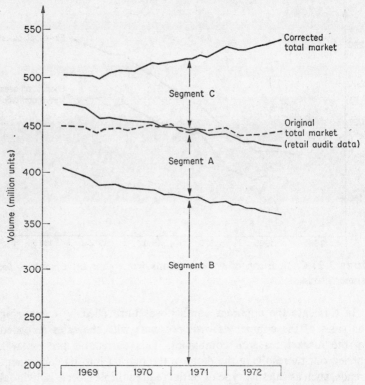

FIGURE 3.3. A consumer market – original and corrected volume trends.

The process of data correction is often quite tedious, for the work must be done in fine detail. In all cases the method of correction must depend on the accuracy of the data that is being compared.

GAPS IN THE MEASUREMENT OF MARKET SIZE

So far the process of data analysis has been discussed as it applies to correcting market research data on a market and its segments. It has been assumed that market research data fairly represents all outlets selling this type of product. In many markets a product may be sold through a very wide range of outlets, and then it is very difficult or expensive to buy data to cover all of them. In this case, not only does data on those outlets that have been measured have to be corrected in some manner, but estimates have to be made for the outlets that are not directly included in the market research data. An example of this process is given below.

A health product. This product was available in grocers, chemists, variety stores and from miscellaneous other outlets. Market research data was available from a retail audit of both the grocers and the chemists. Unfortunately, the data on chemists did not include a major U.K. outlet, the retail chain of Boots Ltd, and was a measurement of sales through independent chemists only. In the past the company had made an estimate of sales through Boots by examining the sales of its own products through that outlet.

The sales through the other outlets not recorded in the market research data had been estimated from management's experience and general knowledge of the market. The sum of all the connected parts gave an estimate of total market size.

Because of the difficulties involved in structuring the market and understanding its trends, it was decided to analyse it thoroughly and build a model to aid interpretation and forecasting. During the definition phase of the model a further set of consumer purchasing data was obtained, and this, in theory at least, covered purchases from all outlets. Detailed analysis of this data showed how much of the product was sold through outlets other than grocers and chemists. With the figures from the original retail audit surveys, a picture of the total market was produced. This process was repeated for each of the three major product types in the market, and each segment was considered independently.

When all these parts were added together, the market was found to be 40 per cent larger than original estimates. In addition, the one segment that was a growth area, and in which new products had been launched over the past few years, was seen to be growing much faster than expected.

Again, the results of the analysis carried out to define the logic of the model gave an early pay-off. The effect of the revelations was a decision to go much more boldly for a larger share of this market, which, at the time of the analysis, was dominated by a multitude of minor brands. Before the analysis was made, the marketing plan called for a volume increase of 15 per cent in the following financial year, but after the analysis a target of 25 per cent was adopted. In fact the volume actually increased by over 30 per cent.

This example is not untypical. The detailed analysis that lies behind any successful market model often yields worthwhile management benefits in its own right. It is sometimes assumed that because market research data is expensive, compiled through a structured sample, and full of interesting computer print-outs, it must be accurate. It is important to realise, however, that the data is based on a sample, and under-reporting is the rule rather than the exception. The degree of the under-reporting can only be determined by thorough analysis, and this takes time.

To emphasize the point, consider the problems that arose in a pharmaceutical market, where it was found that the retail audit data on chemists under-reported sales by 15 per cent. In addition, Boots had a further third of the sales, and the data on grocers was under-reported by 35 per cent. The grocers' sales were approximately half those through chemists, so by taking into account all the various under-reporting factors, the market was 50 per cent bigger than straightforward addition of the retail audit sales would indicate.

DATA ANALYSIS: SEASONALITY AND OTHER CORRECTIONS

Checking, correcting and correlating the various sources of market research and other data are only the first stages of data analysis. It is useful at this point to examine other patterns within the data, such as seasonality. It is now very easy to check market data by using a seasonality adjustment programme on a computer with interactive facilities. This process can allow the model-builder to correct the data for other factors, such as the varying number of selling days in each calendar month.

Determination of the seasonal factors, which may vary from segment to segment of a market, is extremely important. For example, it enables a volume forecast made by the model, generally on an annual basis, to be sub-divided into periodic values for use in short-term planning.

If a market includes seasonal changes, it is always important to determine the appropriate figures so that new data on the market can be seasonally adjusted, and the underlying trend revealed. It can also be useful as an aid to understanding market mechanisms. If the volume data on a market shows a seasonal pattern, how is this reflected in the penetration and consumption rate figures? It is not unusual to find that penetration fluctuates seasonally but consumption rate does not. In other words, the seasonal demand is a reflection of the number of purchasers in the market at different times of the year, but the consumption rate per purchaser is relatively stable.

There are no fixed rules for devising seasonal adjustment methods, but the simplest methods of adjustment are usually the best. Care has to be taken that the observed pattern really is a seasonal one. In one market there were conflicting trends because demand varied with temperature, as well as with the time of the year. In this case it was necessary to work out temperature-correction factors before the seasonal pattern could be isolated.

All the data analysis and correction described so far have been concerned with the volume of the market, because this reflects consumer demand most accurately, but many companies' markets are valued at so many millions of pounds. These amounts are misleading, because the value is the product of volumes and current prices, and if the prices go up, so does the size of the market! But even volume trends can be misleading, as shown by the next example.

Misleading volume trends. In one market a manufacturers' syndicate added up the total output in tonnage as the only way in which every manufacturer could measure his sales on a similar basis. However, the products were not sold by the ton, but in quite small individual units, each one with a selling price in pence. When this data was analysed, it was found that the tonnages fluctuated from time to time, as did the shares of the market held by different product types, which were also calculated by tonnage.

In this market it had been the habit of the manufacturers, when faced with raw material cost increases, to reduce the weight of the product sold to the consumer rather than raise prices. Therefore, the market trends that were measured were more a reflection of manufacturers' behaviour than consumer purchasing habits. It was concluded that the trends in tonnage were not satisfactory indicators of consumer demand, and other methods of analysing this market were devised.

CONSUMER EXPENDITURE ANALYSIS

The comments on the analysis underlying the logic of a model have so far been related mainly to volumes. Consumer expenditure in a market is also a subject for analysis. It is quite common to find that consumer expenditure is related to various economic indicators, such as the retail price index or some measure of consumer disposable income. In many well-established markets there has been no growth in 'real' consumer expenditure, the total expenditure at constant money values having been constant. In such markets a major change, either in product innovation or product pricing, is required to induce dynamic behaviour.

To explain the trends it is sometimes necessary to examine patterns of consumer expenditure in other markets that interact with the one being examined, and to take a wider view of consumer expenditure patterns. For example, the sugar confectionery market should be looked at in conjunction with that for chocolate, and the market for coffee in relation to that for tea.

In another case it was discovered that the major product in a market had held its prices constant, with a consequent decline in the 'real' price, but that the total expenditure in the market had remained constant in 'real' terms. The consumer, therefore, was able to spend more money on new products that had been recently introduced. In this case the marketing manager's weapon to fight the new products was to increase the price of the major product, thus reducing the amount of money available for the new ones.

INCORPORATING CONSUMER BEHAVIOUR FACTORS

Even if the methods that are used for data analysis are comprehensive, and the subsequent correction of market volumes and prices is rigorous, in general this is not a sufficient basis for building a market model. In many consumer markets it has been necessary to relate the volume trends that have been derived to other factors, usually consumer penetration and consumption rate trends. In some markets consumer data may not be available, and so 'per-capita' consumption rates are often considered. Where consumer data is available, it pays to examine patterns in that data. The process is best shown by an example.

Consumer behaviour. A food market contained five segments, and consumer data indicated that some purchasers bought products consistently from more than one segment. They would buy from segments A and B, for example, and, as the data was concerned with measuring the total number of purchasers in each segment, some purchasers were covered more than once. The first step was to unscramble the data so that each buyer was only counted once. In this way the penetration trend of the true number of households buying the product emerged, as shown in Figure 3.4.

An examination of the trend shows that it is made up of two parts, one growing and the other flat. When the flat sections, where there is no increase in penetration, were taken away from the total trend, and all the growth sections were added together, an underlying growth curve emerged. It was then found that the flat parts coincided with price increases in the market. The analysis had determined, therefore, that the increase in penetration followed a basic growth trend, but that it could be delayed by price increases.

This is one example of the results that come from such an analysis. In general terms attempts are made to determine the penetration trends of the users of the product in each segment, and separately to determine the consumption per buyer per year. Factors affecting both are identified, and mathematical relationships between them are established. Once the patterns have been determined, it is possible to use the trends as a basis for forecasting.

One further point worth making is that switching patterns between various segments of the market can often be a useful indicator to future behaviour. Many models of switching behaviour have been determined in theory, but in practice it has been found that their use is limited to those markets where duplication of purchase between segments does not exist.

THE MARKET MODEL SO FAR

It is pertinent to review the steps that have been taken by the model-builder so far. He has based his work on the agreed management specifications, and discussed his findings with the eventual users as his ideas have developed. He has collected together the various categories of data, correlated them, and corrected them for under-reporting or any other similar error. The data has been analysed to

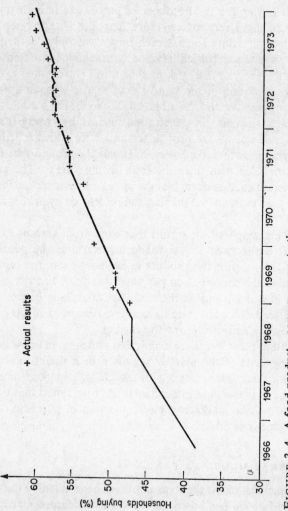

FIGURE 3.4. A food product – consumer penetration.

reveal underlying trends, such as the patterns in consumer penetration and consumption rate. These trends will in turn have been analysed to check them for any correlation with factors such as price increases, general inflation, or perhaps advertising expenditure. In all cases the analysis has been carried out in sufficient detail to reveal the trends, but not in so much detail as to waste time. All statistical relationships that have been found have been discussed and explained in marketing terms. Nothing has been treated as proved unless the marketing managers have agreed.

Each of the component parts of the model has been analysed separately and the model itself is the sum of these parts. In one case the following factors were relevant:

1 The growth in the number of consumers
2 Effects of price changes on the trend of consumer penetration
3 Consumer switching between the segments
4 Duplication of purchase between segments
5 Consumption rate for each segment individually
6 Forecast of household population growth.

The outline logic of this model is shown diagramatically in Figure 3.5. At a given point in time there are a number of existing buyers of the product, and over a period of time, say one year, buyers come into the market, others change their buying habits and switch from one segment to another, and some buyers drop out of the market. From these patterns the segment penetration trends may be forecasted; and when the duplication of purchase between the segments is taken into account, the total market penetration trend can be built up. The forecast of this trend is influenced by the number of price rises in the planning period and the date at which they take place.

Once this work has been done, the penetration trend can be extrapolated, and this in turn affects the segment penetration trends. At this stage all the trends are in terms of the percentage of all households buying the product. These can then be multiplied by a forecast of the number of households, and by consumption-rate trends for each segment, to give segment volume forecasts. Adding up the individual segment forecasts gives the total volume market forecast.

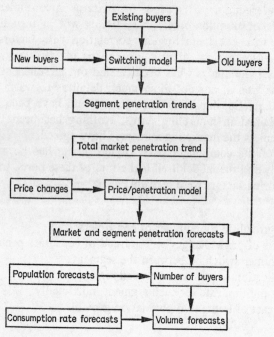

FIGURE 3.5. A consumer market model.

As a check, these figures were divided by the total number of households in the market to give a total market consumption rate. During analysis it was discovered that, although the consumption rates in the three segments of the market were in fact changing, the average consumption rate was constant.

PUTTING THE MODEL ON A COMPUTER

The logic of the market model and the equations that it contains are programmed into a time-sharing computer, which can produce outputs, based on varying management assumptions. In the case under consideration a number of alternative forecasts were produced, according to different pricing assumptions for the future, and different consumption rate patterns. A typical output from the model is shown in Figure 3.6, where the volume forecast for each of the three segments is detailed separately. The print-out has been designed

'SATURN' SEGMENT AND TOTAL MARKET MODEL 2-11-70

SEGMENT VOLUME FORECASTS

YEAR	% HOUSEHOLDS BUYING	CONSUMPTION RATE	SEGMENT VOLUME
		(UNITS/YEAR)	(M.UNITS)

SEGMENT A

1969	13.5	29.0	71.7
1970	13.2	29.5	72.0
1971	12.9	30.0	72.4
1972	12.6	30.5	72.9
1973	12.3	31.0	73.5
1974	12.1	31.5	74.2
1975	11.9	32.0	75.1

SEGMENT B

1969	48.0	38.8	340.9
1970	47.2	37.7	329.0
1971	46.5	37.0	322.3
1972	45.9	36.6	318.9
1973	45.5	36.3	317.8
1974	45.2	36.2	318.0
1975	45.0	36.1	319.1

SEGMENT C

1969	20.3	33.6	125.2
1970	21.7	34.8	140.1
1971	22.9	35.8	153.5
1972	23.9	36.5	165.3
1973	24.7	37.1	175.9
1974	25.4	37.5	185.3
1975	26.1	37.8	193.7

FIGURE 3.6. Market model output.

to be used directly by management, and merely requires copying. The number of figures in each column has been kept down to three, as it has been found from experience that merely printing out long lists of grey figures does not necessarily increase the accuracy of the forecast.

It is important in most market modelling work that the programme is interactive in this way, and that the manager should not just be presented with a set of forecasts based on trends that have come out of the analysis. He should always have the opportunity to override these if he feels that some occurrence could change the trend. It must be borne in mind that the analysis has been carried out on the basis of the historical data, and that in the future the old trends may change and new ones emerge.

The forecasts produced by such a model can remain accurate over a number of years, not because of any particularly clever method of forecasting but more because the analysis has been carried out in sufficient detail to reveal the basic trends, and these correctly represent the marketing forces at work. Such analyses take a certain amount of time, and no market model of any relatively complex market can be built in a period of less than two man-months. Usually they take three or four.

The example just dealt with is relatively simple and straight-forward, but in many cases a market model really helps to structure and unravel more complex markets. This is shown in the following example.

The market for a health product has been mentioned earlier. In this case the market model was built-up from the demand patterns of men and women, considered separately and by age group. An examination of the penetration trends in detail allowed the build-up of a forecasting mechanism, which produced an output as shown in Figure 3.7. Each of the five age groups was considered separately for men and women, and related to forecasts of population, to give a total number of purchasers in the market. The market itself was divided into two segments, based on type of products that were available. The consumption rates trends were analysed and predicted separately. Multiplying the consumption rates by the number of purchasers gives us the total market volume forecast. This is shown in Figure 3.8.

One of the problems faced in analysing this market was that data was available only for independent chemists and grocers, as has been mentioned earlier. The major chemists, Boots, and many other outlets were not recorded directly. And so the analysis was made with the objective of estimating the importance of all the various distribution channels. This allowed the total market volume to be sub-divided into forecasts by outlet type. A typical example of the output, which includes the segmentation split, is shown in Figure 3.9.

```
HEALTH PRODUCT TOTAL MARKET MODEL
-----------------------------------

DO YOU WANT AN EXPLANATION ? NO

FIRST YEAR OF FORECASTING PERIOD ? 73

------------------------------------------------------------------------

HEALTH PRODUCT TOTAL MARKET MODEL                       16/7/73

PURCHASERS & PURCHASE RATES

------------------------------------------------------------------------

POPN. & PURCHASERS       1974    1975    1976    1977    1978
BY AGE & SEX

MALE 13/24 POPN MILL     4.765   4.812   4.890   4.985   5.086
           % PURCHASING  25.5    25.7    26.0    26.2    26.5
           PURCHASERS MILL 1.213  1.237   1.270   1.307   1.347

MALE 25/34 POPN MILL     3.793   3.861   3.923   3.974   4.000
           % PURCHASING  28.5    28.8    29.1    29.3    29.6
           PURCHASERS MILL 1.080  1.111   1.140   1.166   1.186

MALE 35/44 POPN MILL     3.255   3.251   3.235   3.218   3.230
           % PURCHASING  31.7    32.0    32.4    32.7    33.0
           PURCHASERS MILL 1.032  1.041   1.047   1.051   1.066

MALE 45/64 POPN MILL     6.262   6.230   6.203   6.180   6.152
           % PURCHASING  37.8    38.2    38.5    38.9    39.3
           PURCHASERS MILL 2.365  2.377   2.390   2.405   2.418

MALE 65 + POPN MILL      2.855   2.892   2.936   2.976   3.010
           % PURCHASING  30.9    31.2    31.5    31.8    32.2
           PURCHASERS MILL 0.879  0.903   0.926   0.948   0.968

MALE PURCHASERS-TOTAL    6.570   6.669   6.772   6.878   6.985
----------------------
```

FIGURE 3.7. Health product total market model computer output – purchase pattern.

```
PURCHASE RATES
--------------
SOLIDS  UNITS/HEAD P.A. 4.76    4.79    4.81    4.81    4.81
LIQUIDS UNITS/HEAD P.A. 3.96    4.11    4.25    4.30    4.33

------------------------------------------------------------------------

TOTAL MARKET VOLUME FORECASTS
-----------------------------
CONSUMER SALES BASIS

SOLIDS  MILLION UNITS   47.51   48.55   49.46   50.21   50.96
LIQUIDS MILLION UNITS   39.53   41.67   43.69   44.89   45.93

TOTAL   MILLION UNITS   87.04   90.22   93.15   95.10   96.88

------------------------------------------------------------------------
```

FIGURE 3.8. Health product total market model computer output – consumption rates and market volumes.

```
NEW TOTAL MARKET FORECASTS
--------------------------
```

MILLION UNITS

	1974	1975	1976	1977	1978
SOLIDS					
INDEPENDENT CHEMISTS	5.226	5.340	5.441	5.523	5.606
GROCERS	29.456	30.101	30.665	31.130	31.595
OTHER OUTLETS	12.828	13.109	13.354	13.557	13.759
TOTAL-ALL OUTLETS	47.510	48.550	49.460	50.210	50.960
SEGMENTATION SPLIT (%)					
INDEPENDENT CHEMISTS	11	11	11	11	11
GROCERS	62	62	62	62	62
OTHER OUTLETS	27	27	27	27	27
LIQUIDS					
INDEPENDENT CHEMISTS	6.325	6.667	6.990	7.182	7.347
GROCERS	20.160	21.252	22.282	22.894	23.419
OTHER OUTLETS	13.045	13.751	14.418	14.814	15.154
TOTAL-ALL OUTLETS	39.530	41.670	43.690	44.890	45.920
SEGMENTATION SPLIT(%)					
INDEPENDENT CHEMISTS	16	16	16	16	16
GROCERS	51	51	51	51	51
OTHER OUTLETS	33	33	33	33	33

FIGURE 3.9. Health product total market model – segmentation split.

As in the previous example, this particular model was also highly interactive, and the manager could override any of the component forecasts or test out the effect of any change on total volume. For example, with the health product the manager used the model to examine the effects of changing that share of the market held by grocers. It was important to him to know if an increase in total demand would follow a drive to push up sales in grocers. In fact, he found out that this change could be beneficial, particularly if linked to the launch of a new product.

IMPLEMENTATION

USE OF CONTROL SYSTEMS

It has been said that 'control is not an abundance of facts, but knowing what facts to have, and what they mean'. In the case of a total

TOTAL MARKET TRENDS

YEAR	TOTAL MARKET VOLUME NIELSEN CORRECTED		RATIO	CONSUMPTION HOUSEHOLDS	PER RATE	HOUSEHLD % CHANGE
	(MILLION UNITS		(MILLIONS)		(UNITS PER YEAR)	
F65	75.6	93.5	80.8	17.2	5.44	0
F66	79.8	97.6	81.7	17.4	5.6	3.3
F67	81.8	100.2	81.7	7.6	5.70	1.5
F68	90.8	111.1	81.7	17.7	6.26	.9.8
F69	106.3	130.2	81.6	17.9	7.26	15.9
F70	113.0	138.3	81.7	18.1	7.63	5.1
F71	105.2	128.5	81.9	18.3	7.02	-8.0

MOVING ANNUAL TRENDS

F72 PERIOD						
1	108.9	132.3	82.3		7.15	
2	112.0	136.2	82.3		7.36	
3	115.3	140.2	82.2		7.58	
4	117.5	143.0	82.2		7.73	
LE		146.5		18.5	7.92	12.8

FORECASTS

F72		147.1		18.5	7.95	13.3
F73		158.4		18.7	8.48	6.6
F74		164.0		18.9	8.69	2.5
F75		169.5		19.1	8.89	2.3
F76		174.8		19.2	9.08	2.1

2 MONTH NIELSEN PERIOD ESTIMATES

F72 PERIOD						
1	22.8	27.8		18.5	9.02	
2	25.0	30.3		18.5	9.84	
3	25.8	31.4		18.5	10.19	
4	17.9	21.8		18.5	7.08	

FIGURE 3.10. A total market control system – computer output.

market model the analysis isolates the key facts and used them in a model to forecast future demands. All the data and judgement available at the time the model was built are used. The process of measurement in the market is continuous. As new data becomes available, it has to be monitored and checked against the forecasts that have been made. This is the purpose of the control system, an important element in the implementation procedure.

Usually a separate computer program is written to carry out the functions of the control system. It is linked to the market model in the following way. The input to the control system is new data on the market and on the products, collected on a regular basis, normally every two or three months. Various calculations are made by the control system, and its output lists the latest trends revealed by this new data and compares it with the forecast made previously by the market model.

A typical example is shown in Figure 3.10. In this report the historical trends for the market are listed for the previous seven years (as this covered the analysis period), and the latest trends in the current financial year are calculated as a moving annual total. This makes a visual comparison between the historical and the latest estimate (L.E.) very simple. The new trend can also be compared to the forecast for the current year, and the current five-year plan.

The market data for this example was obtained from A. C. Nielsen retail audits. These records and the revised market volumes are listed side by side, so that the manager can be aware of the

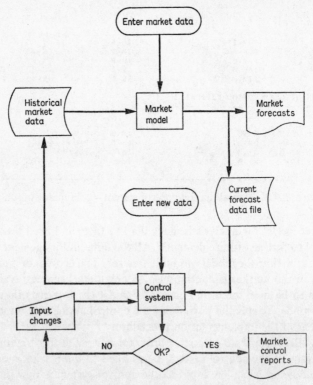

FIGURE 3.11. Overall market model and control system.

correction factor and how this is changing. In this example the ratio was reasonably constant with time. It is useful if these trends are plotted on graphs to give a visual picture of any changes. In addition to the total volumes, the per capita consumption rates have been printed-out, as these were the trends that were used by the market model to make forecasts.

The control system, when used, loads a data file containing the current forecasts automatically. This file was generated by the market model, so that it is a link between two computer programs – one containing the model and the other incorporating the control system. Each time a new set of market forecasts is generated, and accepted by management for planning, it is recorded in this data file. So the control system is always run to monitor the latest forecasts.

When the new data has been checked, and the manager decides that it is satisfactory and no changes are required, say, to the correction factors, the corrected data is fed into another file. This will contain all the historical data on the market, and in its turn is used by the market model when new forecasts are made. The complete system is shown in Figure 3.11.

MAINTENANCE AND DEVELOPMENT

It is normal for the control system to cover more than just checks on market and segment trends. It will often carry out a running check on the seasonal pattern. If this is varying, new factors are calculated and stored automatically in the data file for use by the market model. Also, as in the example based on a health product, any changes to the pattern of distribution will be monitored. The control system should be designed primarily to meet specific management needs and provide key information. This is particularly important, because control systems must prove useful to the manager on an on-going basis. It is only by use that market models remain alive and dynamic enough to aid management planning over a long period of time.

No forecast can guarantee accuracy, even if it is produced by a model! For this reason routine reports comparing the latest trends with forecasts made earlier are essential if management is to have confidence in the assumptions that have been built into the market model. Once this confidence has been established, and the model has proved itself, it will be used to the full, and it will be taken into account when critical decisions are made.

Normally a model that is used intensively will require modification as management becomes familiar with it. Periodic reviews of its operation are therefore needed when the model-builder discusses possible extensions or alterations with the users. With interactive models it is relatively simple to make the necessary changes and to widen the scope of the model as it matures.

INDUSTRIAL MARKETS – AN EXAMPLE

The market models used as examples in this chapter have been mainly concerned with consumer goods, but such methods are equally applicable to consumer durables. The markets for industrial products are more difficult to analyse in detail, often because market research data is generally not available. Some companies play such a small part in markets that are so vast that the market trends are really irrelevant to them. Even in these cases, however, there is a use for some form of econometric analysis, i.e. an analysis that looks at the general trend over a large range of products and examines the change in those trends relative to factors such as capital expenditure, and gross national product.

One example of such a market model for an industrial product specified the analysis of the demand for a basic plastic material in Europe. The factors that were examined included the total capacity currently available in the market, extensions planned by major companies, the price trends of the product, and the general pattern of demand over the previous ten years. Exhaustive analysis of data from many sources revealed two main factors: there were significant and consistent variations between home market and export prices, and total European demand followed a typical economic cyclical pattern.

When demand went up and outstretched capacity, prices rose. This led to investment in more capacity, which came on stream two or three years later, causing a reduction in price because of over-capacity. A strong relationship was found between the changes in price and the changes in excess capacity. Factors dealing with general trends in inflation, in prices and in total demand were built into the model, which enabled a forecast to be made of the future capacity requirements. In this case it appeared that the other major companies in the market were already planning, and had committed money to, excessive changes in capacity. The company decided, therefore, not to invest any more money at that time, because prices were sure to drop.

Two years after the model was constructed one major producer decided to pull out of the market altogether, with the result that the total European capacity dropped by a significant amount. The sudden shortage that developed pushed prices up, and there was under-capacity. Such a dramatic change had not been foreseen, however, and the company had no plan to deal with such a contingency.

This example illustrates both the scope and limitations of market models, and indeed, models in general. The model of the plastic market could have been used to simulate the effect of one or more of the major producers withdrawing from the market. The subsequent effect on prices could have been determined, but management did not use the model in that way.

This is not a reflection on the quality of the model, for model-based systems are no substitute for efficient and imaginative management. Models of markets can be valuable support systems for marketing management, but, like any other tool, they need to be used effectively and creatively.

4. *A Market Model for Predicting Long-Term Demand*

INTRODUCTION – THE VINCENT CASE

Vincent Ltd is a major manufacturer of grocery products in the United Kingdom. The company was founded over a hundred years ago by John Vincent, who patented a new method of processing a food product. Since then Vincent Ltd has expanded through diversification of products and the acquisition of other companies in related areas, such as confectionery.

In 1969, the Vincent family still retained a substantial shareholding in the company, which had maintained its independence in the face of increasing competition. The company was run by a strong team of professional managers, who followed an aggressive marketing policy to sustain and improve their share of many important markets.

At this time Vincent's were marketing a range of twenty products, in three product groups. The major product group was responsible for 40 per cent of turnover and 50 per cent of the contribution to profits. Products in this group were long established, but had little potential for future growth. The second group contained a mixture of old and new products, and was expected to continue to grow steadily for at least another five years. In 1969 this group accounted for 30 per cent of the turnover, and made a 35 per cent contribution to profits. The third group contained products introduced during the 1960s which, after initial losses, were now becoming profitable; 30 per cent of the turnover, but only 15 per cent of the profits, came from this group.

Vincent's decided to initiate a study of Alpha, the major product in the third group, which they considered had an excellent long-term potential. The objectives of this exercise were to analyse the market in detail, to build a model of the market and use it to forecast demand up to ten years ahead, and also to use the modle to assist the marketing management in devising its long-term plans for the product.

This introduction covers the first three out of the seven steps of model-building covered by the main headings in Chapter 3. The emphasis in this case study is on step 4, the definition of the model logic (p. 7), and the analysis behind it.

HISTORICAL TRENDS

Alpha was a confection sold mainly to children and teenagers. Its market was established by a number of products launched during the late 1950s, and Alpha was introduced in 1962. In the ten years up to 1969 the products in this market had been sold through two channels – confectioners, tobacconists and newsagents (C.T.N.s) and grocers. Alpha's distribution had been concentrated on grocers only, an important factor in distinguishing it from its major competitors. Vincent's decided that grocers offered the best long-term prospects for growth, and they already had a sales force that covered all grocery outlets.

A syndicate of manufacturers had been formed for this market, and each one supplied details of its monthly sales to a central pool. When all the sales had been collected, the monthly total was sent back to the manufacturers. This total included sales of all products in the market, whether distributed by C.T.N.s or grocers. From this data total market sales were known exactly, and a good basis existed for the analysis of trends.

In the six years before the model was built (1964 to 1969) the market had grown 250 per cent and Alpha's sales (in tons) by 360 per cent, a high rate of growth by any standard.

The syndicate data gave the volume of sales in tons, but this was not a particularly useful measure, since the products were sold in small units. A great deal of work was put into translating tonnages into meaningful unit volumes, and conversion factors were derived from a detailed analysis of the varieties sold. These established the number of units in each ton. It must be emphasized that these factors were based on the situation at the time the model was first built, and so steps were taken to monitor them and check for any changes.

Table 4.1
ALPHA'S MARKET SHARES

Year	Volume (tons)			Volume (million units)		
	Market	Alpha	Alpha share (%)	Market	Alpha	Alpha share (%)
1964	6,600	880	13·3	52·1	6·3	12·1
1965	8,000	1,180	14·6	63·5	8·4	13·2
1966	9,900	1,540	15·6	79·0	11·0	13·9
1967	11,300	1,930	17·1	89·8	13·8	15·4
1968	13,300	2,440	18·3	105·5	17·4	16·5
1969	16,500	3,310	20·1	130·8	23·6	18·1

A brief summary of the market growth, and Alpha's share, is shown in Table 4.1, in both tonnage and unit terms. As Alpha's weight is greater than the average of the other brands in the market, its share is relatively smaller on a unit basis. The volume trends are plotted in Figure 4.1.

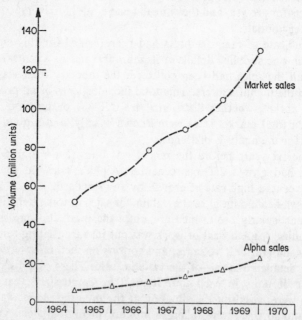

FIGURE 4.1. Market and Alpha volume trends.

THE STRUCTURE OF THE MARKET – MARKET SEGMENTS

The syndicate data contained total sales only, so market research information was bought from a retail audit company to provide data on the sales through grocers. In addition to data on consumer sales and retailers' purchases, this audit included information on price trends, stock levels, and distribution. No reports covering the C.T.N. channel were bought, because Alpha was marketed only through grocers, and it was not intended to change this policy in the near future. However, it was necessary to examine the share of the market held by C.T.N.s, in order to check on the share of sales through grocers.

Other sources of data were examined and the following indicators were found. Apparently the C.T.N. share of the market was 60 per cent in 1967, falling to 40 per cent in 1968 and to 33 per cent in June/July 1969. Assuming that these figures were accurate, it was possible to derive a trend from them; and the relation of the C.T.N. share to the syndicate volumes enabled a volume trend to be calculated.

Both percentage and volume trends were examined closely. It was noted that, although the C.T.N. share had fallen, the rate of decline had slowed down. At the same time the total market volume had increased, so that the C.T.N. volume trend was almost constant. Both trends are shown in Figure 4.2. The assumption drawn about the pattern of sales through the C.T.N. outlet was discussed by the model-builder and management, and was agreed to be reasonable.

It was now possible to subtract the derived C.T.N. volume from the syndicate sales to obtain the grocers' sales trend. When this was compared with that reported by the retail audit data, it was found that there was an under-reporting of 25 per cent in 1966, which had risen to 38 per cent in 1969. With the help of these correction factors, the retail audit data was correlated with that of the syndicate. Figure 4.3 shows the market size, the assumed sales through C.T.N.s, and the grocers' volume trend.

CONSUMER BEHAVIOUR PATTERNS

One problem in this market arose because no continuous consumer panel data had been bought. The only source of information on

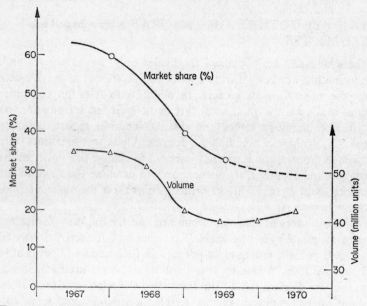

FIGURE 4.2. Sales in C.T.N. outlets.

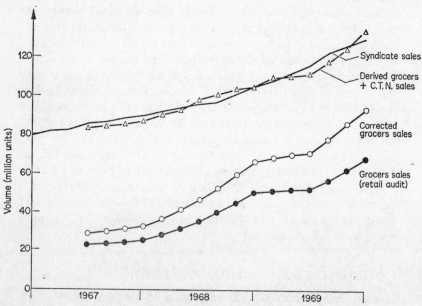

FIGURE 4.3. Actual and corrected market volume trends.

Table 4.2

CONSUMER BEHAVIOUR STUDY

Age of child	No. of children		Age groups	
	Sample	Users	Users	%
1	80	3		
2	85	10		
3	66	15	72	26.6
4	70	20		
5	74	24		
6	74	25		
7	73	26		
8	74	28	121	44.6
9	70	24		
10	67	18		
11–12	138	36	75	27.7
13–15	185	39		
16–20	300	3	3	1.1
Total	1356	271	271	100

consumer behaviour was a 'one-off' study that had been carried out in the first two months of 1968, and had concentrated on a sample of mothers with children living at home. A summary of the results is shown in Table 4.2. The consumption pattern for each age was calculated and the trend expressed as a proportion of the number of users in each group (Figure 4.4), from which it was noted that a peak demand was reached at the age of eight. The study showed also that 80 per cent of the children who consumed products in this market had started before they were eight, and the other 20 per cent had come in between the ages of eight and ten.

Consumption rate patterns were investigated in the study as well as consumer penetration. The investigation showed that a heavy user could be defined as one who bought at least one unit per week, i.e. a minimum of 52 per year. On this basis 35 per cent of all consumers were heavy users and the other 65 per cent were classed as 'other' users. The average consumption for the latter group was about 12 per year. The data arising from the study may be summarized as follows: 20 per cent of all those in the 2–20 years age group

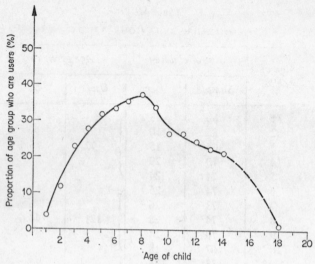

FIGURE 4.4. Consumer penetration by age groups.

ate this product, 24 per cent of those in the 2–5 years age group, 40 per cent in the 6–10 years age group, and 25 per cent in the over-10 age group.

In the period covered by the study syndicate data showed that the average consumption rate per person was 8 units per year. The mean consumption rate calculated from the study was 7·7 units per person per year. Bearing in mind the possible errors with a consumer study of this nature, the fact that both figures were so similar strengthened the case for accepting the validity of the study's results.

MARKET SIMULATION MODEL

Two factors are important in considering this particular market. First, the amount of advertising, particularly on television, had been limited, although the market had been expanding at a brisk rate. Secondly, the market expansion had been steady, with only minor fluctuations at times of economic stagnation in the U.K. Some analysis was carried out into the influences of these two factors on demand, but no statistical correlation was found. Other reasons were needed, therefore, to explain market growth.

The consumer behaviour study indicated that word of mouth

recommendation, between older children and younger children, appeared to be an important factor in persuading children to enter the market for the first time. Assuming this to be true, the following behaviour mechanism was proposed. The consumer population was divided into three age groups – 2–7, 8–13 and 14–19 years. The 8–13 age group bought the most, and was therefore closer to saturation. Since 80 per cent of the consumers entered the market for the first time in the first age group, it was argued that they were probably influenced by the users already in the market. So it was logical to assume that there was a relationship between the number of people in the second age group and that in the first.

The study also showed that no new consumers entered the market over the age of 13. Therefore, it was assumed that the number of consumers entering the market in the second age group was also a function of the number who were already in this group. And as no new users entered the market at all in the third age group, the number of consumers in this group was assumed to be a proportion of those who were in the second age group in the previous period.

It was also assumed that, as more consumers entered the market, a greater percentage of them would consume the product at the heavier rate. The rate of increase in the proportion of heavy users was geared to the rate of change of penetration in the second age group. This model is shown diagrammatically in Figure 4.5.

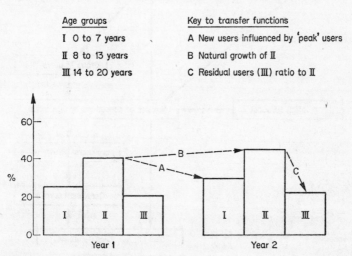

Age groups	Key to transfer functions
I 0 to 7 years	A New users influenced by 'peak' users
II 8 to 13 years	B Natural growth of II
III 14 to 20 years	C Residual users (III) ratio to II

FIGURE 4.5. Market growth mechanism based on consumer behaviour.

Everything was therefore related to the second age group, which had the highest penetration, and was nearer saturation than the other age groups. It was also assumed that growth of users in this age group was proportional to the following ratios:

The difference between the saturation level and the current consumption rate

The difference between the current consumption rate and the consumption rate in the previous year.

These assumptions were expressed mathematically, tested against the trends that had been measured by the syndicate data, and used to derive various parameters. In this way the equations that formed the model were determined.

A flow diagram of the model is shown in Figure 4.6. With a given saturation level for the second age group, and by taking the number

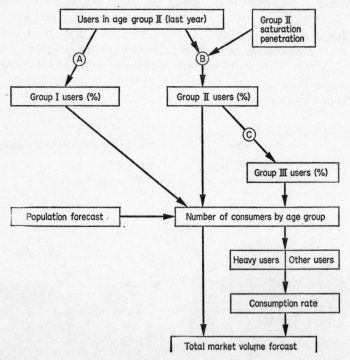

FIGURE 4.6. Alpha's total market model.

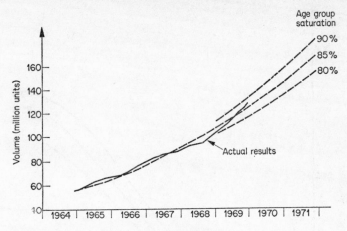

FIGURE 4.7. Short-term market forecast.

of users in the group at a given time into account, the model determines the number of users in the first group as a function of the number of people who were users in the second in the previous year. The number of users in the third group is also a function of the previous number of users in the second who have now moved forward one year. Adding up the number of users gives us a total penetration trend for the market. As the number of users in the second group increases, so does the percentage of those consuming at a heavy rate. The remainder were considered to consume at the average rate of 'other' users, i.e. 12 units/year.

The penetration trends were then related to the expected population growth, to give a number of consumers. The weighted average of the 'heavy' and 'other' user rates gives the average consumption rate. This is multiplied by the number of consumers to give the total market volume. Alternative forecasts can be based on different saturation levels in the second age group. Figure 4.7 shows three such forecasts based on saturation levels of 80 per cent, 85 per cent and 90 per cent. The forecasts are compared with the actual results in the market at the time the model was built.

The model gave a reasonable correlation with the actual sales over the period 1964 and 1969, so it was used with confidence to examine volume trends up to 1980. These forecasts are shown diagrammatically in Figure 4.8, and the corresponding figures are listed in Table 4.3.

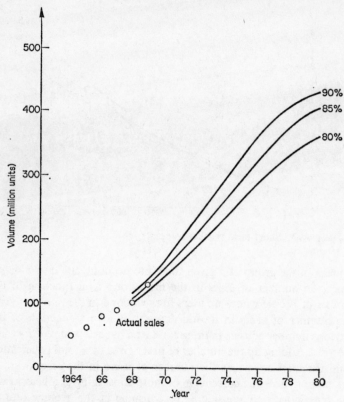

FIGURE 4.8. Long-term total market forecasts.

To the reader unfamiliar with market analyses of this kind the mechanism developed for inclusion in the model may seem complex. It is much less complex than the market for this type of product, however. The model makes that market comprehensible, and produces forecasts that are accurate enough for planning purposes.

POPULATION TRENDS

One factor that will influence future demand in this market is changes in population trends. A problem that arose during the analysis concerned the birth rate, which had started to fall in the U.K., though the government forecasts assumed an upward trend

Table 4.3

TOTAL MARKET FORECASTS
(Million Units)

Year	Actual sales	Forecasts based on age group D saturation units		
		80%	85%	90%
1964	52	52	52	52
1965	64	62	63	64
1966	79	75	77	78
1967	90	89	92	95
1968	106	104	109	116
1969	131	122	131	140
1970		143	155	168
1971		165	182	199
1972		190	210	232
1973		215	239	265
1974		240	269	300
1975		266	298	333
1976		288	324	366
1977		312	352	394
1978		333	375	414
1979		350	396	426
1980		366	408	435

for the future. Detailed analysis of the birth-rate pattern showed that this was unlikely, and revised forecasts of birth rates were therefore made. From these, revised forecasts of the population in the revelant age groups were derived and used in the model.

To give an idea of the problem, Figure 4.9 shows the official government forecasts that have been made in the U.K. at four different times. It can be seen that the birth rate has always been at variance with the forecast. The model was originally constructed in 1969, and since that time the birth rate has continued to fall; but the assumptions made in the population part of the model have proved correct. If anything, they have underestimated the fall in birth rate. Obviously this is an important factor for a manufacturer of products primarily sold to children, because the population for his market will continue to decline.

THE MODEL IN USE

The model was constructed by a model-builder who specialized in this type of project, in conjunction with two members of Vincent's marketing staff. When it was complete, and the programmes were developed, it was presented to Vincent's management team. The concepts in the model were carefully explained. The effects of the assumptions that were built into it were described by showing how the sensitivity of forecasts of future demand varied under changing circumstances.

A presentation is an important stage in the implementation process. In particular, it involves senior management with the model, and helps to obtain their acceptance of the new concept. Without their approval and support, it is very difficult for models to be accepted as an integral part of the marketing planning process.

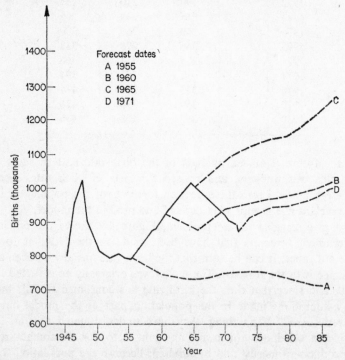

FIGURE 4.9. Actual and projected live births (U.K.).

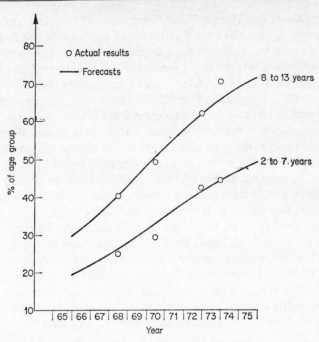

FIGURE 4.10. Comparison of 1969 penetration forecasts and actual results.

In 1969 the model was used by Vincent's to simulate a range of forecasts, and three were chosen as representing the optimistic, expected and pessimistic demand for the market. These became the basis of the marketing plan for the next five years.

The changing pattern of sales in the market, with the decline in the importance of the C.T.N. outlets, led to some further analysis of the growth of the grocers' segment. The increasing dominance of supermarkets was examined in detail, in relation to the number of shops, their size, turnover, and total consumer expenditure on food and confectionery products. Alpha had been traditionally strong in the smaller grocers, and its share of sales through supermarkets was under pressure from new products. As a result of the outlet analysis, a campaign was planned to increase distribution and sales in the larger stores.

As well as using the model to aid planning, a control system was set up to monitor new data on the market as it became available from the syndicate and the retail audit company. This system has been run every two months from mid-1969, and continues in use in 1975.

The model was built around a hypothesis of consumer behaviour derived from a survey carried out in 1968. It was decided that these assumptions should be checked, and another survey was carried out in early 1970. Fortunately it confirmed that the original assumptions were reasonable, and that the model did not need to be altered.

Eventually two further consumer studies were commissioned in mid-1971 and early 1973, and the results of all four were analysed. An example of the comparison is shown in Figure 4.10, where the trends in penetration made by the model in 1969 are plotted with the actual results from the later surveys. It can be claimed, with due modesty, that the original hypothesis was fairly good.

Over the four years from 1969 to 1973 the original market forecasts were hardly changed. By 1973 the sales began to drift away from the forecast trend, and this was corrected by minor changes to the consumer behaviour pattern and revisions to the population trends. The forecasts have been good for four years, and the model is now better than ever as a result of the incorporation of the latest research. Like a good wine, a model matures with age!

5. A Planning Model for an Industrial Company

INTRODUCTION – THE BUILDING BITS CASE

In June 1972 the management of Building Bits Ltd, a division of a group providing materials of various kinds to the construction industry, was approached by consultants offering a service in the construction of business models. After visiting previous clients of the consultants to see a model-based planning system in action, the managing director commissioned a feasibility study, with the following terms of reference:

1 To identify the areas of planning and control in Building Bits Ltd where the construction of models is possible, and where their use would be of benefit to management
2 To outline how the models could work and could extend the existing planning system to improve the quality and flow of information
3 To examine the relative importance of each area, and to recommend a programme of work.

The consultants had asked for a wide brief for their survey, and the managing director had agreed, being convinced by their argument that the starting point for construction of a model-based planning system, whatever its final form should be, could best be determined by looking at all the possible application areas. In discussion with the managing director and some of the more senior members of his management team the consultants had identified the people they needed to see during the feasibility study. These included the accountants and the data-processing manager, in addition to the line managers concerned.

THE RESULTS OF THE FEASIBILITY STUDY

After some five days of interviewing, examining documents, and discussing processes, the consultants concluded that there were two main areas where model-based systems could be used effectively in the planning and control processes of Building Bits Ltd. These were short-term financial evaluation, and long-term planning, in which a model could be used in the determination of strategy. An outline of both was given in the feasibility study report.

After discussions in depth the managing director decided to proceed with the construction of the short-term model, as a first step. The strategic planning model would follow later, if experience with the first were satisfactory.

The consultants estimated that it would take nine man-weeks to construct the model. They proposed to use a commercial time-sharing service in both the development and use phases. Agreement was reached on this basis, and the assignment started in September 1972 with a working session at which the objectives of the assignment were discussed and recorded in detail and a work programme agreed.

THE FINANCIAL EVALUATION MODEL

The construction industry is notoriously volatile, seasonal and cyclical. Its level of activity is closely linked to variations in the national economy.

Building Bits Ltd had a number of plants located throughout the country. All the products in its range were made in much the same way, and the manufacturing process was comparatively simple. Some products could be made in a number of plants. Thus, the company had a considerable degree of flexibility in its operating patterns, which enabled it to meet the fluctuations in demand arising from the volatility of the industry.

In a given demand-supply situation there are usually a number of alternatives open to management, and there was a real need for detailed short-term financial evaluation of the company's position. Means of establishing the sensitivity of profits to factors such as differing levels and patterns of production activity, and to changes in costs, were required. This need led to the decision to start with the financial evaluation model. Essentially the managing director wanted to improve his company's response time when external changes occurred, and to provide himself with a tool for finding better responses.

The model was to be used in two ways. The first was called the routine use. As the sales forecast was updated each quarter, and as costs and prices changed or as new production capacity became available, the changes would be incorporated in the model. The resulting cash and profit situation over the forecast period would then be computed. Secondly, the model would be used to examine the outcome of alternative actions. This was called the simulation use. In short, the model was (1) to provide an updated forecast of results and (2) to act as a planning tool.

THE STRUCTURE OF THE MODEL

The consultant and the managers concerned soon settled down as a team, and began the design of the model. The consultant did most

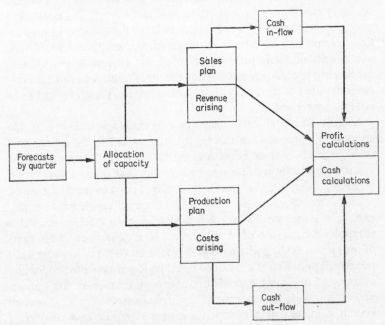

FIGURE 5.1. Model structure.

of the design work, ensuring that he understood the managers' processes in depth, by holding frequent discussions with them. The first diagram produced is shown in Figure 5.1, which shows the logic of the planning process in outline.

The starting point in this figure is the sales forecasts produced by the sales force, by geographical area and by product, for the next five quarters, the first being in monthly detail. The next major step is to allocate production capacity to demand, which results in a sales plan and a production plan. These allow the calculation of the revenue and costs respectively, which in turn lead to profit and cash calculations.

THE CALCULATING LOGIC

The team decided that the existing standard costing system was not flexible enough to calculate profit accurately under certain simulation conditions. Standard costing systems used by most companies are based upon allocations of indirect costs on a largely arbitrary basis, often in proportion to direct labour. For simulation purposes, where the effect of relatively large fluctuations in production volume may have to be investigated, this arbitrary allocation is not a suitable basis for cost calculations. Nor were the existing accounting procedures suitable for the simulation facilities management required of the model. The costing system, therefore, had to be completely revised.

Luckily the cost accountant was in full agreement with the consultant's proposals in this regard, and agreed to the expenditure of a large amount of effort and resources on the revision of the system. The main problem was to keep the indirect and direct costs separate, rather than to allocate the indirect costs to product centres.

The calculations would need to be done in considerable detail, and, in a sense, would not be a mathematical model at all, but a computerized version of existing procedures. However, those parts of the system dealing with cash flow would make use of mathematical relationships, which it was hoped could be found between production output and operating expenditures, between despatches from plants and cash inflow, and in seasonal patterns in both. Thus the revised system consisted of a combination of a computerized version of revised accounting procedures and mathematical models.

From this point, detailed design work proceeded and an intense interaction developed between the consultant and the managers concerned. There was a great amount of work to be done on the definition of costs and their allocation, and the mathematical relationships relating to cash flow had to be found.

Several other design decisions had to be taken during this period. One was the level of detail. A balance had to be struck between a very detailed system providing precison of calculation, and a system using aggregated data, which is easy to use but does not permit detailed manipulations. The key here was to match the level of detail to the desired management processes. In the event it was decided to increase the amount of detail over that envisaged during the feasibility study stage, and the assignment was extended from the original nine man-weeks to fifteen as a result.

It is not unusual, in the construction of model-based systems, to find that the form of the system that evolves during the interaction between the model-builders and the users differs from that outlined during the feasibility study stage. Sometimes this increases the estimated construction time, but the difference should not normally be very large.

Another decision was to make the model modular, so that modification and development would be easy. The team were fully aware that they were not going to produce a system that would last for ever. Changes in the company's situation, and user experience, would inevitably lead to later modifications.

The dual use of the system – routine and simulation – meant that a set of duplicate files was necessary. These were called experimental files. They allowed a manager complete freedom to manipulate and store modified data during simulations without interfering with actual data.

FINAL DESIGN OF THE SYSTEM

The design phase resulted in a detailed specification for the system consisting of six modules that could be used in different combinations to produce the following, on a routine or a simulation basis:

Production, allocation and distribution plans
Product and transport income statements

Plant operating statements
Consolidated net profits
Operating cash flows.

PRODUCTION, ALLOCATION AND DISTRIBUTION PLANS

Figure 5.2 shows this module in outline. The sales forecasts are converted into product despatches by plant for each quarter. Manual control is maintained by the facility to set up and to manipulate an allocation matrix, which allows the whole, or part, of the output of any plant to be allocated to the whole, or part, of any area demand.

This module produces the forms normally used to circulate the production/distribution plans, if these are required, and stores the plans in files for use later in the planning sequence. It can be operated as many times as is necessary to produce what the planner considers

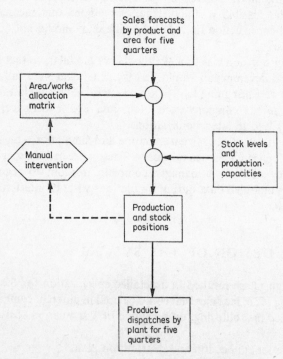

FIGURE 5.2. Production allocation and distribution module.

to be a satisfactory allocation, and allows the introduction of new plant to be simulated.

PRODUCT AND TRANSPORT INCOME STATEMENTS

This module is outlined in Figure 5.3, where the starting point for the calculating logic is product despatches, by plant quarterly, expressed in volume terms. Pricing data, reflecting pricing policy and discount structure, is held in the module, and this, with the volume data, leads to income calculations. The products can be collected by customers from the plants, or can be delivered by the company to construction sites. Naturally the price of delivered products is higher, and the module calculates separately the income arising from the haulage operation. Variable selling expenses are deducted from gross income to arrive at the value of sales.

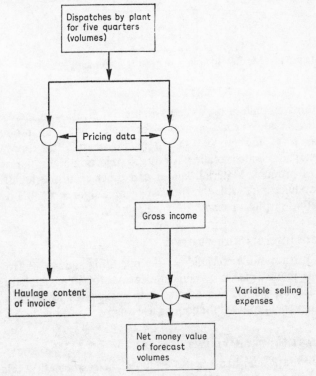

FIGURE 5.3. Product and transport income module.

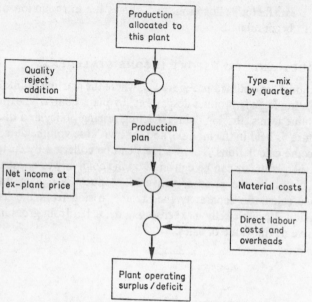

FIGURE 5.4. Module for plant operating statement.

PLANT OPERATING STATEMENTS

The third module in the system, Figure 5.4, deals with the costs of production and operating profit for each plant. The production figures from the module shown in Figure 5.2 (the production module) are inflated to allow for quality rejection and split down by type of product. Material, labour and other costs are handled by the module, and, with the forecast income figures, enable a plant operating surplus or deficit to be calculated.

CONSOLIDATED NET PROFITS

The fourth module consolidates the operating statements from the various plants, makes certain adjustments for inter-plant transfer, and deducts selling and administration expenses to arrive at the divisional net profit for the coming five quarters.

OPERATING CASH FLOWS

The first task here had been to establish the mathematical relationships between invoicing and payment, which was called the payment delay factor. The lag between purchasing and payment was investigated in a similar manner. Monthly figures were used in the analysis, five years back data being available.

Remarkably stable monthly seasonal patterns became evident, as did consistent payment delay factors. An on-line analysis package was used to investigate seasonality. The two modules handling cash inflows and outflows are shown in Figures 5.5 and 5.6 respectively. It will be seen that VAT is treated separately.

During this phase of the work, the consultant was in very close touch with the divisional accountants.

Although the description and the diagrams of the modules make them seem simple, many difficulties had to be overcome, particularly as regards definitions, before the simple structure and logic shown

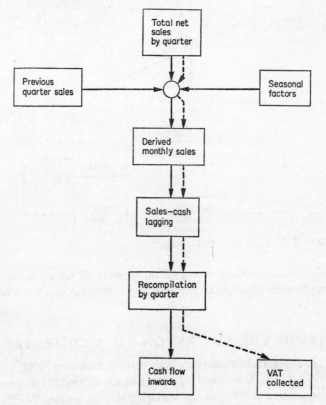

FIGURE 5.5. Cash inflow module.

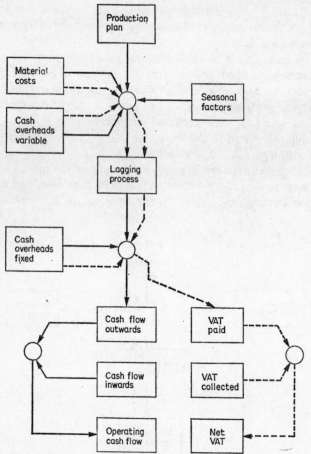

FIGURE 5.6. Cash outflow module.

evolved. The consultant described the process as 'taking the costing system to pieces and putting it back together again in a more useful way.'

PUTTING THE SYSTEM ON TO A COMPUTER

Programming then took place, the various modules being written in FORTRAN. A terminal operating at ten characters per second was linked to a commercial time-sharing service. During this stage a member of the company's data-processing staff worked with the consultant on the system, in the process becoming familiar with the programme, the file structures, and the operating methods. An operating manual was produced, as was a summary report for management use.

BRINGING THE SYSTEM INTO USE

Once the usual presentations and discussions about the facilities available on the system had been completed, it was considered ready for use. The close cooperation in the team during the construction stage meant that very little formal training was necessary.

The model is now used on a routine quarterly basis to evaluate the sales forecast. The most important part of the quarterly run is a check of the sales forecast against planned production. If it is found that the expected demand is likely to exceed available supply, management must plan accordingly.

The model has been used to examine the effects of various pricing policies, within a framework established by projected increases in material and other costs, and government legislation regarding price increases. A further use has been to evaluate a new production plant. This plant was set up on paper with various associated costs and revenues and its effect on divisional performance simulated.

SYSTEM DEVELOPMENT

The management had decided to use the system for one year before investigating how to develop it further. In the event, it was decided to transfer the complete system from the commercial time-sharing service to the company's own in-house computer. This machine did not have the powerful interactive facilities of the time-sharing service, but it was considerably cheaper – a cost advantage considered to be greater than the operating disadvantages.

Later the long-term planning model was constructed, by a design team consisting of one consultant and two members of the company staff. The experience gained during the operation of the financial evaluation model proved valuable in the design of the long-term planning model. The company had then successfully completed the first two phases of its carefully thought out system-development programme.

6. *Product Planning*

The models discussed so far have been used mainly in strategy formation. In many companies strategic planning is considered by managers only once or twice a year, and day-to-day activities are much more concerned with shorter-term planning for individual products. Many models have been built for use in product planning, ranging from simple designs using simulation techniques to complex models based on detailed analysis of a product's performance within its market environment. All models, however, whether simple or complex, are developed to assist a manager whose decision-making processes are complicated by the number of factors he has to consider.

Most managers tend to concentrate on those factors they understand and to ignore those they do not. Often there is insufficient time for the manager to consider all the alternatives, and he rarely has the chance to test his theories in the market place. In consequence, a manager often has to make a series of decisions about a product when he has neither the time nor sufficient data to analyse his problems in depth.

This is where a model, even a simple one, can be of tremendous practical value. It can help the manager to make better decisions, by providing a framework for the decision processes, and by skilful use of a model the manager can test the outcome of the alternative plans that he has created.

A PRODUCT PLANNING MODEL

The simplest form of product planning model is that based on the simulation technique. Here the model represents the logical steps taken by the manager when he is making his decision. An example will show how this works in practice.

THE MARKET

One major feature of a market for a consumer company was the large number of products that were available, and the considerable variation in pack sizes for each product. Before the model construction was started, the managers had stated that very many factors could influence demand, some of which were the following:

Loyalty to manufacturer
Taste performance (i.e. recipe variations)
Pack characteristics
Retail price
Product weight
Brand advertising
Consumer promotions
Display factors, such as the number of facings on a shelf, and their location in the shop
Trade acceptability, in terms of special deals discounts, or special trade advertising and promotions
Manufacturers' trading policies
Credit terms
Frequency of representative's calls.

Some of these factors are independent, some are interdependent, and others are related to the market or to changes in demand for types of product over time. Some factors may have more importance to certain age groups than others. The impulsive nature of consumer purchasing behaviour in this market made point-of-sale activities very important.

The management believed that the identification of the potential consumers for this brand was very important. It was known that the success of many brands in this market had been largely dependent on the correct identification of the potential consumers, and a marketing effort directed precisely at them. The market was approaching saturation and new products aimed at specific targets tended to increase sales at the expense of existing brands.

The marketing management's major problem was to determine which of the wide range of products should be promoted, and how the sales of these could be increased at the expense of competitive products, without affecting sales of other products in their own range.

A PREDICTIVE MODEL?

The first approach to providing a model-based system to support management's decision-making processes was an attempt to construct a predictive model. This would have enabled management to determine how a product would perform in the market place, given certain levels of activity in the factors that affected the demand for it. This approach was abandoned, however, after the initial investigations. The principal reason was the lack of detailed data, as it was found impossible to isolate and quantify the factors influencing demand using the data that was available. There were many products in the market, and the consumer purchasing habits were not clearly defined. The model-builders concluded that it was unlikely that market research data in sufficient depth would ever become available. They therefore started to look for an alternative approach.

A SIMULATION MODEL

The model-builders turned again to their analysis of management processes. They had hoped to establish in the model a series of equations that would help the management's judgement of product performance, but though they could not achieve this, management still had to judge what performance was likely under given conditions. Given this limitation, what assistance could a model provide? Detailed discussions with management followed, and a specification of management requirements was drawn up.

The model was to play a role in both the planning and control processes of management. It would be related to the annual planning and control cycle, and would deal with one year only. Its fundamental job was to take a number of inputs concerning marketing, selling and cost factors, and to work out their financial implications. In the planning mode the model would be used to simulate product performance for a financial year, the management exploring a range of plans by altering the inputs in accordance with their judgement. In the control mode the model would be used to monitor the variances in performance during the year.

The output of the model would be in four columns of figures. The first column would represent the budget for the year, the second column a performance resulting from unchanged volume but changed costs, the third the performance that would result from no change in costs but changed volumes, and the fourth the performance resulting from the latest information on both sales and costs.

There was to be one page of output for each pack size, and one for the product in total. All inputs were to be variable, and the effect of changes in inputs was to be shown in terms of change in contribution to profit.

THE DEFINITION OF MODEL LOGIC

Work started on this basis, the logic and definitions being agreed in detail. For example, factory costs were established, by pack, under the following headings:

Material costs
Wages
Fixed and variable overheads
Production losses
Processing costs
Packaging.

Other areas included cost of media advertising by product, below-the-line expenditure, tax rates and distributors' margins. All data was assembled by pack, by month.

The logic of the model is shown in Figure 6.1. It can be seen that the model is interactive, the manager being asked to give his approval in three places (the boxes marked 'OK?'), and to make changes to either the base data or the product data if he is not satisfied.

THE COMPUTER PROGRAMMES

The base data was held in a file that was loaded automatically when the manager ran his programme. The first step was normally to check the cost and volume data held in this file, and to enter any changes that were necessary.

Figure 6.2 shows part of the conversation between the manager and the machine during the early stages. The machine asks for the product type, and the manager tells it number one. He then establishes the period of time with which he is to be concerned. In this case he wanted to look at the data for 1971, starting at month ten. The first data the computer printed was the present tax level, which

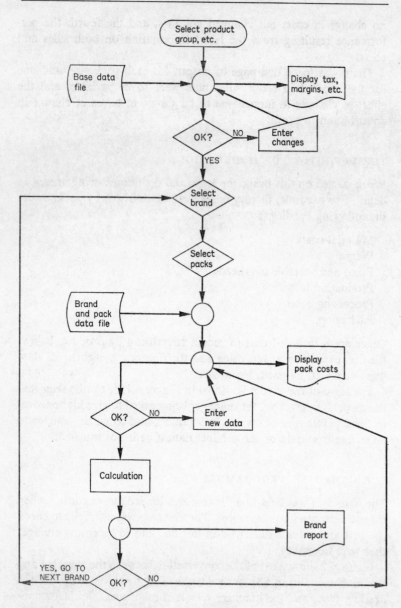

FIGURE 6.1. A product simulation model.

```
WHICH PRODUCT AREA CODE?
     PC=1

ENTER BASE YEAR,PERIOD NUMBER,RUN NO
     FY=71
     PD=10
     NRUN=1


PRESENT TAX LEVEL          18.0

ANY CHANGES THIS YEAR?
     ANS=YES

SPECIFY PERIOD OF CHANGE AND NEW LEVEL
     PER=10
     TAX[4,10]=16
     PER=END

PRESENT TRADE MARGIN       33.0

ANY CHANGES THIS YEAR?
     ANS=YES
     PER=11
     TM[4,11]35
     PER=END

HOW MANY BRANDS THIS RUN?
     NB=1

WHICH ONES(IN ORDER OF SELECTION)?
     B[1]=1
BRAND NO.
BRAND NO.   1

HOW MANY PACKS?
     NP[1]=5

WHICH ONES(CODES)?
     PP[1,1]=1
     PP[1,2]=2
     PP[1,3]=3
     PP[1,4]=4
     PP[1,5]=5
```

FIGURE 6.2. Product simulation model – an example of the initial data input to the program.

was 18 per cent. It then demanded, 'Any changes this year?'. The manager answered, 'Yes'. Then the computer asked him to specify the period of the change, and the new tax level. The manager typed 'period 10' and gave the new tax rate as 16 per cent. The next question was 'period' once again, so that further rates could be entered if required. By typing 'end' the manager told the machine that the latest tax rate, of 16 per cent, was to apply for the rest of the year.

A similar process is then followed for trade margins, where the present level is 33 per cent. Once again the computer demands,

'Any changes this year?' The manager answers, 'Yes', and changes the margin to 35 per cent for period 11.

So far, only general data, applying to all products, had been checked. The next stage was for the manager to select the brand products he wished to be investigated, within the product group originally chosen. When the computer demanded, 'How many brands?', the manager replied, 'one', and when asked which brand (brand=product), he selected brand number three. The machine then asked, 'How many packs?' The manager typed 'five', and then gave the code numbers of the various packs. The manager had the choice of selecting any product he wished within the product group. For these products he could choose any pack. Having made the selection, he could then revise any of the costs, which were stored on the computer file.

An example of the question and answer approach, used for making cost changes, is shown in Figure 6.3. The first question was 'Any cost revisions for material costs?' The answer was 'Yes'. Within that cost group there are a number of component costs that can be examined. These are listed by the computer. The manager decided that he wished to change the material costs (MATS), and the variable (VOHS) and fixed (FOHS) overheads. For the ingredient costs he selected the particular ingredient by code number, the period of the change, and then entered the new cost as a percentage change. This procedure was repeated until all the latest costs had been entered. Finally, the latest estimates of sales by pack were entered for the remaining periods of the current year.

The figures show the model being set up to compute the financial outcome of changes in sales forecasts and costs, which are then compared to the original budget estimates, set up before the start of the financial year.

Figure 6.4 shows the output for two of the packs. It is in six columns:

Column	*Data*
1	Budget estimates (drawn up in the planning process)
2	Budget volumes and latest costs
3	Budgeted costs and latest volumes
4	Latest volumes and latest costs
5	The variance between column 4 (i.e. the latest estimates), and column 1

```
RE. EDIBLE MATERIALS, ANY COST REVISIONS?
        ANS=YES

MATERIALS, WAGES, VARIABLE O/HS, FIXED O/HS OR LOSSES?
        MATS=YES
        WAGES=NO
        VOHS=YES
        FOHS=YES
        LOSS=NO

INGREDIENTS
ENTER INGRED. CODE, PERIOD AND % CHANGE
        CODE=1
        PER=10
        PCH[10]=-10
        PER=END
        CODE=3
        PER=11
        PCH[11]=15
        PER=END
        CODE=END

VARIABLE O/HS
BY PACK OR BRAND?
        PACK=YES
        PACO=2
        PER=11
        PCH[11]=5
        PER=END
        PACO=5
        PER=11
        PCH[11]=5
        PER=END
        PACO=END

FIXED O/HS
BY PACK OR BRAND?
        PACK=NO
        PER=11
        PCH[11]=10
        PER=END
```

FIGURE 6.3. Product simulation model – an example of cost changes.

6   Variance percentage (the ratio between column 5 and column 1)

Full interpretation of these results requires a knowledge of the accounting definitions and procedures of the company. However, it can be seen that on Pack Number 2 there had been an increase of 1·4 per cent in both tonnage and consumer spend. Sales income is arrived at by deducting tax payable and trade margins from consumer spend. In this case there is an increase of 1·6 per cent in sales income, which is followed through to an increase in gross contribution of 3 per cent, after cost changes. Pack Number 3 shows a similar picture.

When the outputs for the individual packs had been printed, the computer consolidated the total for the product. The output is shown in Figure 6.5. Normally the manager selected the particular pack output he wished to examine, and then tested the effects of changes of pack strategy within the total. For example, if demand for larger packs was found to be increasing at a faster rate than was assumed in the budget figures, this would affect various costs but might not increase revenue for the total product. The manager used the model to simulate changes to any combination of costs or

	1	2	3	4	5	6(%)
PACK NO.2						
PRICE	3.5	3.5	3.5	3.5		
WEIGHT PER UNIT	20.1	20.1	20.1	20.1		
OUTERS(000'S)	2255	2255	2288.1	2288.1	33.1	1.4
TONNAGE	3797.8	3797.8	3853.5	3853.5	55.7	1.4
CONSUMER SPENDING	3788.4	3788.4	3844.0	3844.0	55.6	1.4
TAX PAYABLE	451.6	437.2	458.2	443.1	-8.5	-1.9
TRADE MARGINS	827.9	839.8	840.1	852.2	24.3	2.8
SALES INCOME	2508.9	2511.5	2545.7	2538.7	39.8	1.6
INGREDIENT COST	1043.6	1026.9	1058.9	1041.4	-.22	-.2
OTHER VARIABLE COST	187.3	187.4	190.0	190.2	2.9	1.5
TOTAL VARIABLE COST	1230.9	1214.3	1248.9	1231.5	.6	.1
GROSS CONTRIBUTION	1278.0	1297.2	1296.8	1317.2	39.2	3
FIXED FACTORY COST	116.0	116.3	116.0	116.3	.2	.2
GROSS MARGIN	1162.0	1180.9	1180.7	1200.9	38.9	3.2
GROSS MARGIN(%)	46.3	47.0	46.4	47.1	.8	1.7
BELOW LINE SPEND	13	13	13	13	0	0

	1	2	3	4	5	6(%)
PACK NO.3						
PRICE	5	5	5	5		
WEIGHT PER UNIT	37.5	37.5	37.5	37.5		
OUTERS(000'S)	2648.7	2648.7	2647.7	2647.7	-1	0
TONNAGE	8314.1	8314.1	8311	8311	-3.1	0
CONSUMER SPENDING	6356.9	6356.9	6354.4	6354.4	-2.4	0
TAX PAYABLE	757.8	733.7	757.5	733.4	-24.4	-3.3
TRADE MARGINS	1389.3	1408.8	1388.7	1408.6	19.3	1.4
SALES INCOME	4209.9	4214.4	4208.3	42412.5	2.7	.1
INGREDIENT COST	2293.5	2256.9	2292.7	2256.1	-37.5	-1.7
OTHER VARIABLE COST	300.2	300.4	300.1	300.3	0	0
TOTAL VARIABLE COST	2598.8	2557.3	2592.8	2556.3	-37.4	-1.5
GROSS CONTRIBUTION	1616.1	1657.1	1615.5	1656.2	40.1	2.4
FIXED FACTORY COST	182.0	182.5	182.0	182.5	.5	.3
GROSS MARGIN	1434.1	1474.1	1433.5	1473.7	39.6	2.7
GROSS MARGIN(%)	34.1	35.0	34.1	35.0	.9	2.6
BELOW LINE SPEND	13	13.8	13	13.8	.8	5.8

FIGURE 6.4. Product simulation model – output for two packs.

	1	2	3	4	5	6(%)
OUTERS(000'S)	7592.2	7592.2	7598.1	7598.1	5.9	.1
TONNAGE	18767	18767	18749	18749	-18.0	-.1
CONSUMER SPENDING	15829	15829	15826	15826	-4.0	0
TAX PAYABLE	1887	1819	1886	1819	-67.7	-3.7
TRADE MARGINS	3459	3514	3458	3513	53.9	1.5
SALES INCOME	10483	10495	10480	10493	9.8	.1
INGREDIENT COST	5176	5083	5179	5078	-97.9	-1.9
OTHER VARIABLE COST	735	736.	735	736	.7	.1
TOTAL VARIABLE COST	5911	5819	5906	5814	-97.2	-1.7
GROSS CONTRIBUTION	4571	4676	4573	4678	107.1	2.3
FIXED FACTORY COST	520	521	520	521	1.6	.3
GROSS AMRGIN	4051	4154	4054	4157	105.4	2.5
GROSS MARGIN (%)	38.6	39.6	38.7	39.6	1.0	2.4
BELOW LINE SPENDING	65	67	65	67	2.8	4.1
MEDIA SPENDING	65	63	65	63	-2.0	-3.2
TOTAL PROM. SPENDING	130	130	130	130	.8	.6
NET MARGIN	3921	4024	3924	4026	104.6	2.6
NET MARGIN(%)	37.4	38.3	37.4	38.4	1.0	2.5

FIGURE 6.5. Product simulation model – brand total output.

volumes, as well as checking the effects of latest estimates of sales forecasts. He used it for more than one product, because the budgeting procedure that had been built into the model was similar for all the products within the company. The manager was able to examine the effects of actual and possible changes in prices, costs, or volumes on a continuous basis.

The relationships between these factors were not contained in the model, but left to his judgement. However, the effects on contribution to profit of changes to any or all of the factors could be determined in a matter of minutes. The manager's thinking was no longer constrained by problems of time and detail.

PRODUCT RESPONSE MODELS

In the last example a simulation method was used because it was found impossible, in that market, to determine specific relationships such as that between price and sales volume, between various factors and their effects. This was mainly because of difficulties with the data and with the way measurements had been made by market research companies.

Often market research or other comprehensive data is not available at all. It may be that the market size cannot be determined, or is irrelevant as far as a particular product is concerned. In those circumstances it is possible that the only data is the company's own sales figures for a product, its prices, the cost of manufacture and the marketing and selling expenditure. Despite this lack of data, the manager has to make the usual decisions about the product: he has to make sales forecasts, to allocate marketing and selling effort, and in some way to relate changes in marketing and selling effort to changes in volume.

Even in the absence of comprehensive data, a model can sometimes help the manager. One approach is to try to derive a relationship between particular factors, let us say selling effort and sales, even though there is no specific data available on the effects of changes of one on the other. In this situation a response function can be used.

A response function is a curve relating changes in one factor to changes in another. In the absence of good data it is only possible to construct such curves from a manager's knowledge and judgement on the behaviour of a particular product. As an example, consider the construction of a response curve that relates the calling rate of a salesman to the average level of sales achieved as a result of those calls. This could apply to a 'detail man' (a salesman) calling on a general practitioner to outline the merits of a particular pharmaceutical product. The sales that result from this type of activity are measured by the number of prescriptions written for that product. Alternatively, the situation could be that of a representative calling on a wholesaler to obtain orders for a product.

As an instance of this approach, consider an industrial product. Analysis of sales showed that the average call rate on purchasing companies had been four a year, and the average sales achieved in the past year 800 units per company. On a sheet of graph paper sales were plotted vertically and call rate horizontally. Appropriate scales were chosen, and one point was plotted on the graph to correspond with the current calling rate and order level.

The sales manager was asked, 'What would happen if the representative called eight times a year?' He replied that the sales would probably reach about 1,200 units. In other words, he estimated that doubling the calling rate would increase sales by 50 per cent. That was the second point on the graph.

The next step was to consider what would happen if the representative did not call at all. Would sales fall to zero? This was most unlikely. In this example it was considered that about 200 units would be ordered. Finally, the manager was asked, 'What would happen if the call rate were halved, to two visits per year?' He estimated that the order level would be about 450 units.

There were now four points on the graph, and a curve was fitted to these (Figure 6.6). From this curve it is, of course, possible to read off the order levels at any calling rate. The 'S'-shaped curve shown is typical of many that occur in marketing.

The balance between call rate and sales solved part of the problem, but costs had also to be considered. It was decided to take into account the marginal profit from selling each unit of volume, the fixed costs, and the variable cost of each call. Using the computer to calculate the equation of the response curve, and reading off the sales levels at the various call rates, one can calculate the marginal profit generated by the extra sales. The fixed cost and the cost of making the calls are deducted from this profit, to give the marginal increase in contribution that results from the increased sales. If this contribution is divided by the number of calls made, the contribution generated by each extra call and each additional order can be calculated (Figure 6.7).

The computer has the advantage, as always, of being able to carry out the calculations accurately and speedily, and to take care of the financial calculations involved. This, in turn, enables a

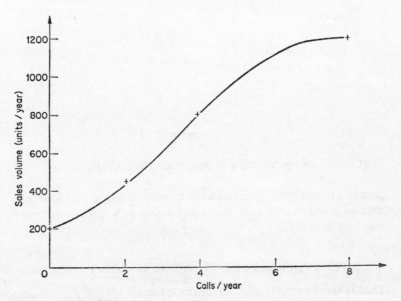

FIGURE 6.6. A response curve.

Call rate	Sales volume	Turnover	Production costs	Selling costs	Contribution	
					Total	Per call
Calls / year	Units	£	£	.£	£	£
0	200	2000	2800	0	-800	
1	300	3000	3200	100	-300	-300
2	450	4500	3800	200	500	250
3	600	6000	4400	300	1300	433
4	800	8000	5200	400	2400	600
5	1000	10,000	6000	500	3500	700
6	1100	11,000	6400	600	4000	667
7	1180	11,800	6720	700	4380	630
8	1200	12,000	6800	800	4400	550

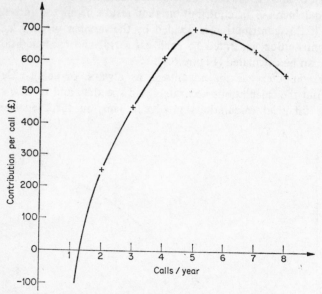

FIGURE 6.7. Response curve of contribution to call rate.

manager to test more alternatives in a given time than would otherwise be possible. The next case study shows how a response curve was used in practice.

DUBOIS PHARMACEUTICAL COMPANY

The Dubois Pharmaceutical Company is a small company in France, specializing in the manufacture and selling of ethical pharmaceutical products to general practitioners and hospitals. The company started ten years ago, when Claude Dubois obtained a licence for distributing a new ethical product from a company in England. This licence allowed him exclusive distribution of the product in France.

Initially he built up a small sales force, and started detailing the product to doctors. His success in this enterprise allowed him to obtain a manufacturer's licence for France. So he obtained a small factory, and at the same time entered into further licensing agreements with other manufacturers for some other products.

By 1968 Claude Dubois was handling a range of twelve important pharmaceutical products and a few minor ones. He employed twenty-five men in the factory. His sales force had, by this time, built up to a total of seventeen men: twelve detailed his products to the general practitioners, his original area of activity, and the other five were employed for detailing solely to major hospitals.

In 1968 he obtained a licence for a new product, Gamma, which was aimed at the hospital market. His small hospital sales force did not enable Claude to promote the drug as widely as a major company could have done, but in spite of this limitation, he managed to increase sales steadily over the first two years. By the end of 1968 the revenue from this product had reached 500,000 francs.

It is normal practice for pharmaceutical products to be classified into a product class that comprises drugs with apparently similar therapeutic qualities. Most of the rival products had been manufactured for over twenty years, and there was some doubt in the minds of the doctors as to whether they were particularly effective. Until Gamma's arrival on the scene their only choice was to select from the existing range.

Dubois had a small company and could not afford to buy detailed data from the market research companies who audit the sales of drugs used in hospitals. Even if the company had had this data, it was unlikely that it would have been of much use, for the sales of Gamma by the end of 1968 were still very small, and would hardly have appeared in any market research sample.

In 1969 the results of some clinical trials on Gamma were published in a leading French medical journal. These compared the therapeutic qualities of Gamma with the other products on the market, and showed that, in certain circumstances, Gamma was considerably more effective. It had certain therapeutic qualities that the other products lacked. This report excited Claude Dubois. It was the first

4

time, in any country, that this product had received such independent validation.

It also gave him a problem. How much effort should be placed behind Gamma, and in particular, should he hire some extra salesman to 'detail' this product to more hospitals? If Dubois had been running a large company it is likely that he would have switched the extra resources from other products for a limited period of time, to see whether an increased detailing effort would have led to increased sales. For Claude Dubois this solution was not possible, however, as he still had to maintain the detailing efforts on his other products.

THE DUBOIS MODEL

He decided to analyse the market for Gamma, and to use the results of the analysis in a simulation model, which could then be used for testing alternative marketing policies. The objective was to decide the level of detailing support that would be required.

The market for Gamma could be divided into three major segments. The first segment comprised major hospitals, which had their own pharmacies and could order the product direct from Dubois Laboratories; the second, wholesalers and major pharmacies which, in the main, supplied those hospitals that did not have their own pharmacies; and the third, sales to other pharmacists, who stocked Gamma for use by general practitioners.

It has already been mentioned that there was no market research data for the product and, therefore, the analysis was based on Dubois's own sales history.

By the end of 1969 the major proportion of Gamma's sales was to the major hospitals, which comprised 60 per cent of the total, and a further 10 per cent went to major pharmacists. The growth pattern in sales over three years is shown in Figure 6.8, where both the monthly sales and the three-monthly moving average are plotted.

Some 300 of the major hospitals had their own pharmacies, and were therefore able to order the product direct. Figure 6.9 shows the number of hospitals by size in France. It also shows the number of hospitals allowed to order direct. Naturally, these tend to be the larger ones.

It was decided to analyse Gamma sales to individual hospitals, in order to build up a pattern for all the hospitals. The hospitals

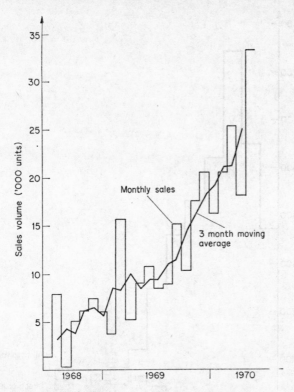

FIGURE 6.8. Gamma sales.

were classified into three groups. The first consisted of regular users, which had ordered Gamma at least twice in a six-month period; the second, restored users, which had previously ordered on a regular basis, dropped out for a period of six months or more, and had subsequently ordered again; and the third, drop-outs, or hospitals that had stopped ordering for a period of six months or more, and from which no further orders had been received.

It must be noted that orders were received for batches of 50 or 100 units of Gamma at a time. The batch would be retained in the hospital pharmacy, whence Gamma would be drawn by the doctors as it was required. Therefore, the ordering pattern by a hospital could be expected to be erratic.

By the end of 1969 thirty-five of the 300 direct-ordering hospitals were regular users, and the average consumption rate was 100 units

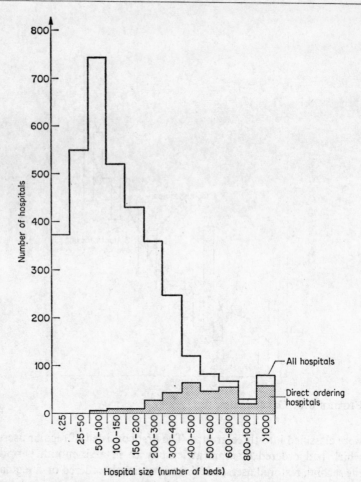

FIGURE 6.9. The number of direct-ordering hospitals compared to the total number of hospitals.

per regular user per month. The trends in penetration and consumption rate are shown in Figure 6.10. At the time of the analysis, therefore, penetration had been low, probably between 3 per cent and 5 per cent of all hospitals. Figure 6.10 shows also the extrapolation of the penetration and consumption rate trends to give a forecast of potential sales of Gamma over the next five years.

This gave an outline of the potential market. Obviously, the potential was very high, because Gamma's current penetration was

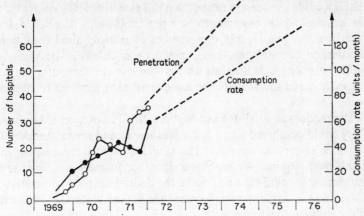

FIGURE 6.10. Gamma – hospital penetration and consumption rate trends.

low. In order to test alternative plans for the next five years, a simulation model was built on the basis of this analysis, in which the following assumptions had to be made:

1 The number of major hospitals
2 The number of other general hospitals
3 The number of special clinics
4 The penetration of major hospitals by regular users
5 The penetration of major hospitals by lapsed users
6 The penetration of other general hospitals by regular users
7 The penetration of other general hospitals by lapsed users
8 The penetration of special clinics by regular users
9 The penetration of special clinics by lapsed users
10–15 The consumption rates in each of the hospital groups
16 The number of visiting days in a year
17 The visits per man per day
18 The call frequency – the number of visits per annum to major hospitals, to other hospitals, to special hospitals.

At this stage, the analysis had not shown a specific relationship between calling frequency by the representative on hospitals and subsequent orders for Gamma, but it had produced the average calling rate on hospitals that had their own pharmacies. From this information certain assumptions were made. For example, it was assumed that it would be necessary to maintain this rate in order to ensure that the hospital would continue to be a regular Gamma user. Then, by reversing this relationship, the number of men required to obtain the desired hospital penetration could be calculated. The analysis yielded certain guide lines, which were used in the form of a simple response curve to calculate the number of men required to obtain certain results.

The model stored all the assumptions listed above, on a data file. They could be altered when a run was made, and new assumptions could be entered as required. The model calculated the number of detail men required for each year in order to meet the necessary number of hospital calls and make the desired hospital penetration. There was a 'rounding up' procedure to calculate the required effort to the nearest man.

The model did not end here. It also considered the cost aspects of selling the product, the following assumptions being required in the data file:

The first year cost per man
The follow-on cost, per man, per year
Gamma selling price.

From this data the cost of detailing was calculated. At this stage it was sufficient to express the cost of detailing as a percentage of cost of sales, and to calculate the contribution from Gamma to its production costs and profits. A typical set of detailing assumptions is shown in Figure 6.11, with the number of visiting days per annum, the visits per man per day, and the desired call frequencies to major hospitals, other general hospitals, and special clinics.

In the model the number of detail men is rounded up or down to the nearest number of total men, so that the call frequency is modified accordingly, as shown in Figure 6.12, which gives a complete output from the model. The number of detail men is actually the number of extra men required over and above the existing sales force that is visiting hospitals. It was calculated that one man of the five in the existing force was detailing Gamma at any one time, but in the Gamma model the number of men was assumed to be the men required to detail Gamma on a full-time basis.

A whole series of simulations were made using the model, and they showed that the number of men would have to rise from the current level of five to at least ten or eleven men, and that the extra men

No.	Assumptions	No. of Entries
11	No. of Major Hospitals	1
12	Other General Hospitals	1
13	Special Clinics	1
21	Penetration – Major Hospitals – Regular	5
22	– Lapsed	5
23	Other Generals – Regular	5
24	– Lapsed	5
25	Special Clinics – Regular	5
26	– Lapsed	5
31	Consumption – Major Hospitals – Regular	5
32	– Lapsed	5
33	Other Generals – Regular	5
34	– Lapsed	5
35	Special Clinics – Regular	5
36	– Lapsed	5
41	Visiting days per annum	5
42	Visits per man day	5
43	Call frequency (visits PA) – Majors	5
44	– Other	5
45	– Specials	5
46	First year cost per man	5
47	Following cost per man year	5
48	Part time calls per month	5
49	Cost per part time call	5
51	PACK A selling price per unit	5
51	PACK B selling price per unit	5
61	Consumption (units/month)	
	Major Hospitals – Regular	5
62	Other Generals – Regular	5
63	Special Clinics – Regular	5
71	No. of Prescriptions P.A.	5
72	Average prescription size (units)	5

FIGURE 6.11. Assumptions required for the Gamma model.

```
REVISED ASSUMPTIONS
-------------------
                        YEAR    1       2       3       4       5
                                -----   -----   -----   -----   ------
NO. OF DETAIL MEN               3       3       3       3       3
CALL FREQUENCY (VISITS PA)
  1) MAJOR HOSPITALS            15.05   15.05   15.05   15.05   15.05
  2) OTHER GENERAL HOSPITALS    0       0       0       0       0
  3) SPECIAL CLINICS            0       0       0       0       0
DOCTORS VISITS PER MONTH        200     200     200     200     200
```

```
===========================================================================

                        YEAR    1       2       3       4       5
                                -----   -----   -----   -----   -----
SALES (THOUSAND F)
==================

PACK A
------
  1) MAJOR HOSPITALS-REGULAR     378     604     936    1260    1555
  2)               -LAPSED       6       7       7       8       9
  3) OTHER GEN HOSPS-REGULAR     0       0       0       0       0
  4)               -LAPSED       0       0       0       0       0
  5) SPECIAL CLINICS-REGULAR     0       0       0       0       0
  6)               -LAPSED       0       0       0       0       0
                                -----   -----   -----   -----   -----
TOTAL REVENUE                    384     611     943    1268    1564


PACK B
------
  7) MAJOR HOSPITALS-REGULAR     28      32      60      69      98
  8) OTHER GEN HOSPS -REGULAR    0       0       0       0       0
  9) SPECIAL CLINIC -REGULAR     0       0       0       0       0
 10) SALES THROUGH DOCTORS       25      25      25      25      25
                                -----   -----   -----   -----   -----
TOTAL REVENUE                    437     669    1028    1362    1688
                                -----   -----   -----   -----   -----
COST OF DETAILING
-----------------
1ST YEAR MEN                     0       0       0       0       0
TRAINED MEN                      195     195     195     19U     195
PART TIME FORCE                  34      34      34      34      34
                                -----   -----   -----   -----   -----
TOTAL COST OF DETAILING          229     229     229     229     229
                                -----   -----   -----   -----   -----
% OF SALES                       52      34      22      17      14

===========================================================================
```

FIGURE 6.12. Gamma model output.

would have to spend their entire time detailing Gamma, if the product was to be maintained effectively. One simulation showed that, on this basis, revenue would increase from the current level of 500,000 francs per annum to 4,500,000 francs.

It was obvious that Gamma had considerable potential, and Claude Dubois decided to put all five of his existing force on to a 'crash' programme of detailing at once. During a period of three months, in early 1970, all the major hospitals in France were visited at least once by the hospital detail force, which presented only Gamma to the doctors.

THE DUBOIS MONITORING SYSTEM

Dubois could not afford to have his small force concentrating on one product for a longer period than three months, so that it was essential to obtain as much information as possible from this short exercise. A monitoring system was therefore set up, and a second model was built to carry out the calculations.

Basically the monitoring system tracked the sales of Gamma to the direct ordering hospitals. It was decided to concentrate on these because they were likely to remain the major sector of the market for at least the next two or three years. Each month the sales of Gamma, by hospital, were entered into the model, and these were added automatically to the data file, which contained the previous years' sales history of each of the 300 direct-ordering hospitals.

The monitoring model was designed to be run and be updated at monthly intervals, generally in practice within the first week of a new calendar month. The model produced five reports, in which the sales figures were corrected for the number of invoicing days per month. It should be noted that, at the time the model was set up, no seasonal pattern in demand had been established. The reports were as follows:

1 *Hospital performance.* In this report the hospitals were classified into four groups: (a) the regular users, or hospitals that had ordered some form of Gamma at least twice in the previous six months; (b) the new users, or hospitals that had ordered in the current month but had never used Gamma before; (c) the restored users, or hospitals that had ordered in the current month but had not used Gamma in the previous period of six months, although before then at least one order had been placed; and (d) the drop-outs, or hospitals that had ordered Gamma six months before but had not re-ordered.

The report listed the number in each of the groups for the current month.

2 *The number of sales in units.* For each of the pack types, the report gave the six months' previous sales, the current month's sales, the percentage change on last month, the sales in the current

financial year to date, and the predicted sales for the next six months.

3 *The amount of sales in francs.* The same as Report 2 except that the data was in francs instead of units. The conversion was carried out on the basis of the current selling prices of Gamma.

4 *Penetration trends.* These were given for each of the hospitals, in each of the groups listed in Report 1. The output shows the last two months' penetration, the current month's figures, the percentage change on last month, and the predictions for the next three months.

5 *Consumption rates.* This report is very similar to Report 4, except that it contains the consumption rates. Consumption rate was defined as the sales in a month divided by the number of regular users in that month.

```
ENTER SELLING PRICES
301:  29.0
302:  10.0
303:  25.5
304:  11.5
```

===

SALES REPORT

SALES TO DIRECT ORDERING HOSPITALS
(CORRECTED FOR INVOICING DAYS)

MAY   1973

UNITS

		301	302	303	304
		---	---	---	---
HISTORY					
DECEMBER	1972	1	1174	10	0
JANUARY	1973	7	1073	67	0
FEBRUARY	1973	93	2050	44	0
MARCH	1973	7	1459	23	0
APRIL	1973	13	1004	40	0
THIS MONTH		2	3041	34	0
% CHANGE ON LAST MONTH		-84	202	-14	0
YEAR TO DATE		148	14139	390	5
PREDICTIONS					
JUNE	1973	36	2050	32	0
JULY	1973	40	2190	31	0
AUGUST	1973	44	2329	30	0
SEPTEMBER	1973	48	2468	29	0
OCTOBER	1973	51	2608	27	0
NOVEMBER	1973	55	2747	26	0

===

FIGURE 6.13a. Gamma monitor sales report – volume trends.

```
                    SALES REPORT

PENETRATION AND CONSUMPTION

MAY     1973

                          REG     NEW     RES     DROP
                          -----   -----   -----   -----
PENETRATION
-----------
        MARCH   1973      35      5       0       5
        APRIL   1973      36      4       2       3

THIS MONTH                35      5       1       3
% CHANGE ON LAST MONTH    -2      25      -50     0

PREDICTIONS
        JUNE    1973      40      2       1       2
        JULY    1973      42      2       1       2
        AUGUST  1973      44      2       1       2


=====================================================================

                          A       B       C       D
                          -----   -----   -----   -----
CONSUMPTION
-----------
(UNITS/MONTH - CORRECTED FOR INVOICING DAYS)
        MARCH   1973      0       41      0       0
        APRIL   1973      0       27      1       0

THIS MONTH                0       86      0       0
% CHANGE ON LAST MONTH    0       218     -100    0

PREDICTIONS
        JUNE    1973      0       50      0       0
        JULY    1973      0       51      0       0
        AUGUST  1973      0       52      0       0

=====================================================================
```

FIGURE 6.13b. Gamma monitor sales report – penetration and consumption rates.

Figure 6.13 gives a typical set of outputs for May 1973, with examples of Reports 2, 4 and 5.

In addition to these five reports, a report could be obtained for individual hospitals on request, giving the sales pattern over the previous twelve months. This enabled the manager to examine in detail each of the 'drop-outs' or restored users, as required each month. It was used to help decide where the detail men should call during the following month.

After a period of six months, following the increased detailing effort to the major hospitals by the total sales force, a stable relationship was derived in the form of a response curve linking the consumption of Gamma to detailing effort and hospital size. This curve related consumption per bed to the number of interviews per

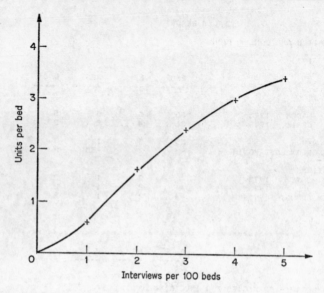

FIGURE 6.14. Gamma response curve between call rate, hospital size, and unit sales.

bed (Figure 6.14), and was a major improvement over the assumptions that had been made previously between calling rate and consumption. Claude Dubois decided to build this relationship into the simulation model. This allowed him to use the model in a second way, to examine questions such as 'If I hire four men, what level of sales would I achieve and what would be the return on the investment?'

In fact, he used the model to test a further ten alternatives, the results of some of which are shown in Figure 6.15. The simulations considered the effects of four different levels of selling effort by one, two, three or four extra men. This force could be sent to major hospitals only, to major hospitals and clinics, or to all hospitals. A typical output for one of these simulations is shown in Figure 6.16.

What can be learnt from this use of the model? A major point is that a straightforward analysis of the sales figures enabled a model to be based on the extrapolation of the current trends. This was extended by taking into account the response of Gamma sales to increased marketing effort. Dubois stated, once he had seen the results of this analysis, that he had not considered Gamma's potential to be so great. Without the model Gamma certainly would have been less successful.

The second major benefit was to relate this potential to the required effort in detailing, particularly the investment in the number of men required. Initially this was carried out by assuming certain relationships between consumption rate and sales. Later, these assumptions were replaced by more specific relationships derived from experimental data.

For a small company such as Dubois Laboratories it was a major decision to increase the size of the sales force, particularly just for

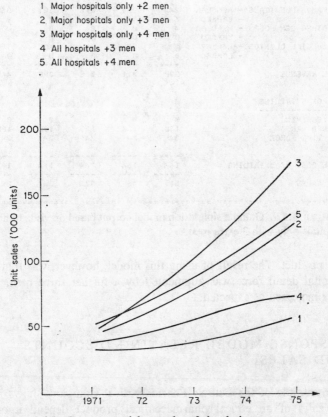

FIGURE 6.15. Gamma model – results of simulations.

```
                    DETAILING SIMULATION
                    --------------------

REVISED ASSUMPTIONS
-------------------
                    YEAR    1       2       3       4       5
                            -----   -----   -----   -----   -----
NO. OF DETAIL MEN            2       2       2       2       2
CALL FREQUENCY (VISITS PA)
  1) MAJOR HOSPITALS         8.21    8.21    8.21    8.21    8.21
  2) OTHER GENERAL HOSPITALS 0       0       0       0       0
  3) SPECIAL CLINICS         2.74    2.74    2.74    2.74    2.74
DOCTORS VISITS PER MONTH     200     200     200     200     200

==================================================================

                    YEAR    1       2       3       4       5
                            -----   -----   -----   -----   -----

SALES (THOUSAND FRANCS)
-----------------------

  1) MAJOR HOSPITALS - REGULAR  240     267     296     327     360
  2)                 - LAPSED     6       7       7       8       9
  3) OTHER GEN HOSPS.- REGULAR    0       0       0       0       0
  4)                 - LAPSED     0       0       0       0       0
  5) SPECIAL CLINICS -REGULAR    24      37      49      63      79
  6)                 - LAPSED     0       0       0       0       0
                                -----   -----   -----   -----   -----
TOTAL REVENUE                   270     311     352     398     449


COST OF DETAILING
-----------------
1ST YEAR MEN                     0       0       0       0       0
TRAINED MEN                    130     130     130     130     130
PART TIME FORCE                 34      34      34      34      34

                                -----   -----   -----   -----   -----
TOTAL COST OF DETAILING        164     164     164     164     164
                                -----   -----   -----   -----   -----
% OF SALES                      51      45      38      34      29

==================================================================
```

FIGURE 6.16. Gamma simulation model output based on visits to major hospitals only with 3 extra men.

one product. The result of using this model, however, was that the hospital detail force was augmented by a further three men, and sales increased as expected.

RESPONSE MODEL RELATING DISCOUNTS AND SALES

The example of the Dubois Pharmaceutical Company shows how the sales of an ethical pharmaceutical product depend upon a limited number of outlets. This situation obtains with many products, and is a factor that many companies have to take into account in planning. For example, in the marketing of food products in the U.K. a number of supermarket chains are taking an increasing share of the total consumer expenditure on grocery products, and becoming increasingly dominant in the marketing of food products.

Many food companies deal directly with these major companies on a national basis. They are no longer able to rely on the abilities of their sales force to call on the managers at a local level. In such a situation a model was used to aid pricing decisions for national accounts for a product called Kappa.

THE KAPPA CASE

Analysis of the sales statistics for Kappa showed that the following were the top nine key accounts:

Allied Grocers
Co-operative Wholesale Society
Fine Fare
Mace
Moore's
Spar
Tesco
V.G. Shops
Sainsbury's

In 1972 53 per cent of Kappa sales went to these nine outlets, and by 1973 this had risen to 56 per cent. Relating this increase in share to the total share that the major outlets had of all grocery products, it was predicted that the top nine key accounts were likely to have at least 65 per cent of all Kappa sales by 1980. In 1973 it was decided to analyse the situation.

The food manufacturing company's sales figures were available by major outlets, and the data on the top nine key accounts was extracted. The data listed the sales in tons for each month, and also the price per case at which the product was sold. The data was in the form of records kept by the company's data-processing computer. Each time a deal was set up with a multiple chain, a special code was allocated, so that the amount of the product sold, and the price at which it was sold, under this specific deal, were listed. It was therefore possible to isolate from the data the amount of product sold under normal terms of trading, and that sold subject to a special deal.

A typical trading pattern over a year for two of the outlets, Chains A and B, is shown in Figure 6.17, where the two diagrams are those in which special deals took place; it is immediately obvious that sales with trade dealing were considerably higher than those under normal terms. The reason is that under the terms of the deal the price advantage enjoyed by the multiple chain was normally passed on to the consumer in the form of lower prices. In the months when there was no trade dealing the average sales were calculated.

In the case of Chain B, for example, the average sales per month were 16 tons over the period shown. Two deals took place in this

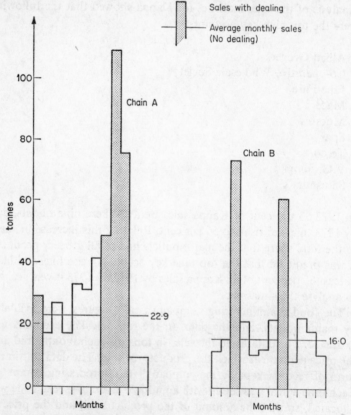

FIGURE 6.17. Kappa sales in two major accounts.

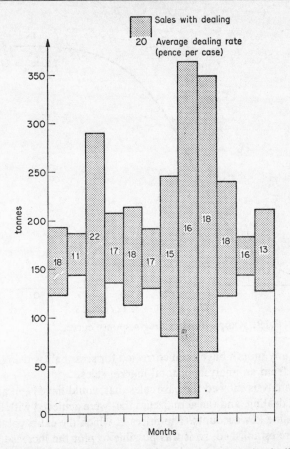

FIGURE 6.18. Kappa sales – the amount sold by trade dealing (key accounts only).

period, with sales of 62 and 75 tons respectively. It was argued that the sales over 16 tons per month were increases due to the deal.

This process was repeated for each of the nine key accounts, and a total volume breakdown was obtained. Whenever a deal took place, the increased volume was isolated and the price at which the deal took place was determined. Adding up the effects over all nine accounts gave the pattern shown in Figure 6.18. The shaded areas represent the additional sales generated by trade dealing, and within these the prices per case below normal terms are also shown. The

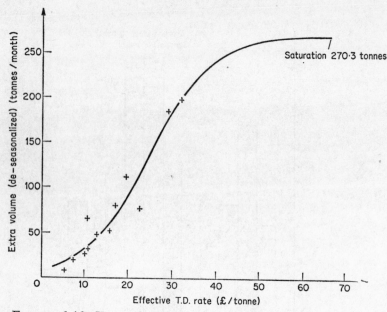

FIGURE 6.19. Kappa trade dealing response curve.

sales in any month have been corrected for seasonality, using factors derived from an analysis of total market sales.

This analysis showed the base sales that would have been achieved without dealing, and the actual sales that were achieved with dealing, for the nine key accounts. The prices at which the extra volume was sold were established, so it was possible to plot the increase in sales above the average level with the decrease in price that had been offered (Figure 6.19).

The curve that was fitted to these points is a typical response function. Statistically the 'best fit' of the curve to the actual points gave a saturation level of about 270 tons per month. In other words, however attractive the trade deal, sales should not be expected to increase by more than 270 tons per month over all nine accounts.

A simple simulation model was built to incorporate this relationship. It was used by the managers to decide on the level of dealing required by individual accounts. The total budget required for trade dealing was then generated, and the expected extra sales target was set. In the model the response curve was normalized, i.e. it was made unit-less. The following definitions were used to rearrange the data. The normalized volume was defined as the total volume sold in a given period divided by the average sales level in the same period. The normalized price was the effective price obtained (with dealing) divided by the normal list price. This reverses the direction of the curve as shown in Figure 6.20, where the vertical axis is normalized volume and the horizontal axis is normalized price. For a normalized price of less than one the produce is being sold at a discount.

Consider how this curve works in practice. If the current price for Kappa is £300 per ton, and the discount being offered is £30 per ton, then the normalized price is (£300 − £30) divided by £300, which equals 0·9. From Figure 6.20 a normalized price of 0·9 gives a normalized volume of 2·3. If the account in question has average sales of 30 tons per month, then, under a 10 per cent price deal, the volume increase should be 2·3 × 30 or 69 tons.

Alternatively, if it is desired to increase the sales to a particular outlet by 50 per cent – in other words, the normalized volume would be 1·5 – the curve shows that the effective price should be 0·945. Relating that to the actual price at the time the deal was made would give an indication of the specific discount to be offered.

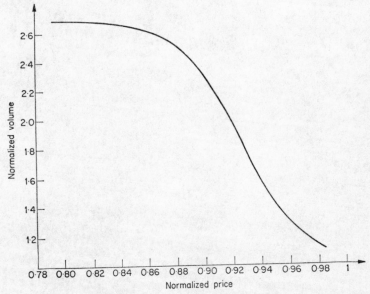

FIGURE 6.20. Kappa top 9 national accounts – normalized response curve.

SUMMARY

In this example, as in the case of the Dubois Pharmaceutical Company, only data readily available within the company was used. In both cases market research data was either not available or not appropriate. From the company's own data, useful trends were derived, which were of considerable benefit to management in making decisions. By using models in this way managers can obtain added benefit from data that they already have available. This type of model can be built relatively quickly.

Managers are often surprised at the amount of really useful information that is concealed in the data with which they are familiar. Once they find how effective a simple modelling exercise can be, they often ask for other areas to be investigated. They are then well along the learning curve that will take them to the effective use of business models.

7. *Market-Share Models*

INTRODUCTION

In earlier chapters models that can produce a better understanding of the mechanisms at work in a market have been described. It has been shown how they can be used to examine a market's potential, and how the manager can monitor and predict changes with their help. Such models provide a firm base for marketing planning and control.

In a sense models of markets define the ground over which the marketing battle will be fought. The armies used in the battle are the competing products, and the weapons marketing factors such as price and advertising. It is with the sales performance of their products that marketing managers are rightly concerned.

The sales of consumer products can be influenced by such factors as advertising, promotional activity, direct selling effort, distribution, packaging and price. Marketing managers in industrial companies will include the factors of reliability, after-sales service, and ease of maintenance.

Where a wide range of factors affecting performance exists, the sales data for a product, by itself, is insufficient to enable a model of the product to be built. Market research data is also needed. Without it, it is impossible to relate changes in the various factors affecting a product to changes in sales, particularly under competitive conditions.

It is under these conditions that market-share models have been constructed, with the objective of relating the market share of a product to the factors that could influence changes in that share. For example, the model could attempt to answer the question, 'What would happen to market share if advertising share were increased by 20 per cent?'

A considerable number of market share-models have been built, and it has been shown that it is often possible to identify and quantify effectively the relationships between the influencing factors. Such a model can easily be differentiated from the simple simulation approaches described in Chapter 6, where all relationships were based on judgement. In a market-share model the objective of the analysis is to find quantifiable relationships. Once again, the best way to describe the process of analysis, and the construction of the model, is by example.

THE DRAKE COMPANY

Consider the example of two food products, manufactured and sold in the U.K. by Drake Products Ltd, in the same market.

The primary source of data, for both the market and the products, was a retail audit of food stores. Total consumer sales were examined over a four-year period, and it was discovered that the market was saturated in volume terms. The audit data was available on a two-monthly basis, and an analysis over the four-year period showed a steady seasonal pattern. The market had a trough during May/June and reached a peak in September/October. Over the period 1968–70 the mean seasonal factors were the following:

January/February	1·07
March/April	0·97
May/June	0·86
July/August	0·96
September/October	1·11
November/December	1·03

These factors were used to convert an annual demand into forecasts of sales by two-monthly periods.

Drakes's two products were Beta, a major product with large sales, and Delta, which had much smaller sales. A comparison made between the ex-factory sales of both products and the retailers' purchases, as reported in the retail audit, showed that the average under-reporting factor was 1·24 for Beta and 1·18 for Delta.

In this market a major product, Titan, was manufactured by a rival company, and there were also a considerable number of 'own-label' brands. To correct the retail audit, it was decided to apply the volume ratio derived for Beta to the consumer sales for Titan. This was justified on the grounds that both were major brands and had similar distribution characteristics. The correction factor for the 'own-label' brands, which were sold under a range of names, depending upon the outlets, was assumed to be similar to Delta's, as both types of product had a limited distribution.

Some consumer-panel data, also available on this market, was used to carry out further checks between the sales by class of outlet recorded by the retail audit and that measured by the consumer panel. This check confirmed that the correction factors were good enough for the purposes of further analysis.

The original (retail audit) and corrected values of the market size are shown in Table 7.1. It was necessary to check and correct the total market data in order to calculate the true market shares

Table 7.1

MARKET VOLUMES (Million Units)

	1969	1970	1971	1972
Original Market	3·00	3·02	3·01	2·98
Corrected Values	3·43	3·46	3·48	3·62

for the products in the market. Since the correction ratios were not the same for all the products in the market, the market shares differ from those reported in the retail audit data. The figures for the four years in question, based on corrected consumer sales volumes, are given in Table 7.2.

The Table 7.2 identifies the problems that faced Drake. Both Beta and Delta had been losing ground to Titan, a serious development in a saturated market. It was noted also, on the surface at least, that Titan's market-share growth had slowed in 1971. Similarly, the decline of Delta's share had slowed.

The corrected audit data was now in a form that could be used to carry out an analysis of the performance of the products in the market.

Table 7.2

	1969	1970	1971	1972
Beta	31·0	28·4	28·8	27·4
Delta	12·0	11·4	11·6	10·1
Titan	22·6	26·2	29·2	30·0
Own label	34·4	34·0	30·4	32·5

THE ANALYSIS OF DRAKE'S PRODUCTS

It is interesting to note that the main method used to unravel the data was multiple regression analysis, a powerful mathematical method that allows cause and effect relationships between two or more factors to be determined. It must be used with extreme caution by model-builders, in case they misunderstand the significance of the results, in management as well as in statistical terms.

The initial analysis was concentrated on attempts to relate Beta's share of the total market to various factors, including consumer price, price differential with other products, shop distribution, sterling distribution,* retail stock levels, advertising expenditure, and share of advertising expenditure. In all cases it was impossible to find a reasonable statistical relationship between any of these factors and market share. With such a few words is a considerable amount of work written off! During this part of the analysis a number of other relationships were tested, but none of these yielded useful results either.

The model-builder had arrived at an impasse. There was no doubt that Beta's share had declined, but the analysis, to date, had explained nothing. Further discussions with the marketing managers led to the idea that the market should not be treated as a single market but as two parts interacting with each other. The main part of the market, it was thought, consisted of the three major branded products – Beta, Delta and Titan. The other part of the market comprised the other products, 90 per cent of which were 'own-label'. It was decided to carry out a new analysis, based on this definition of market structure.

'ALL OTHERS' SHARE

Initially the 'all others' share of the total market was examined and analysed against the following factors:

Consumer price (pence per pack)
Price differential, i.e. the difference between the branded products on average and the 'all others'

---

* Shop distribution, weighted by shop turnover. A product is said to have 50 per cent shop distribution if it is in half the shops selling that type of product. If the shops stocking it have 60 per cent of the turnover, it has 60 per cent sterling distribution.

Sterling distribution of the own-label products (per cent)
Total advertising expenditure for the major products (£'000).

After a number of regression runs it was found that a major factor affecting the 'all others' share was price differential, i.e. its price advantage over the major products. The analysis also showed that 'own-label' distribution, and advertising expenditure by the major brands, expressed as a four-month moving-total, explained further variations in share. The relationships were expressed for marketing management in the following terms:

1 Each penny per pack price advantage gives 'own-label' products a 5 per cent increase in market share
2 A 1 per cent increase in 'own-label' products' sterling distribution gives them a $1\frac{1}{2}$ per cent increase in market share
3 An increase of £100,000 in advertising expenditure by the major products over a four-month period would reduce 'own-label' share by 1 per cent.

From these relationships it might be considered that the share was not very sensitive to advertising, but it should be remembered that it was not unusual for £400,000 to be spent on the major products in a four-month period.

A comparison between the 'own-label' market share and that calculated from the equation is shown in Figure 7.1, which illustrates also the price differential and consumer price trends over the same time period. Not all the fluctuations in market share have been explained. This is often the case in an analysis of product performance, as there are some factors which cannot be quantified. (The goodness of fit was 77 per cent in this case.)

Following this analysis, the 'own-label' products were eliminated, and the sales of Beta, Delta and Titan were then recalculated as shares of the 'branded sector' of the market. For the remainder of the analysis 'market share' means share of the branded sector of the market. On this basis, at the end of 1972, the shares were Beta 40 per cent, Delta 15 per cent, and Titan 45 per cent.

DELTA'S SHARE

It was decided to examine Delta first. Its market share had been steady, at around 17 per cent, for a number of years. It then dropped

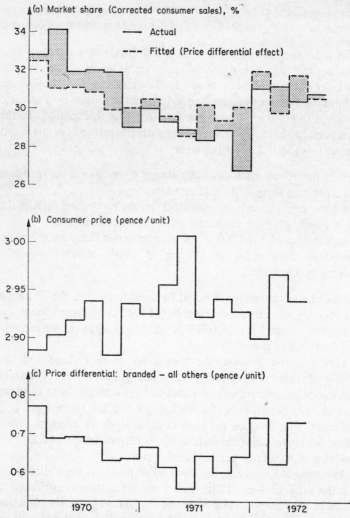

FIGURE 7.1. 'Own-label' market share.

suddenly to 14 per cent at the end of 1971. It remained at the 13–14 per cent level before rising to 15 per cent at the end of 1972. From the market research data it was found that advertising expenditure had been cut at the end of 1971, and that this cut corresponded with the drop in market share. Advertising of the other two products was not cut at that time, so that Delta's share of advertising expenditure also fell. One of the factors in Delta's favour was a price advantage over its major rival, Titan. This had been eroded for an eight-month period between the end of 1971 and early 1972.

The results of the analysis for Delta showed that its share of the market was determined by

The amount of money spent on advertising over a four-month period.

The share it had of total advertising expenditure

The difference between Delta's and Titan's price.

This explained 89 per cent of the variations in Delta's market share. It took some time to carry out this analysis, no less than twelve models being tested before the final one was chosen.

When the calculated and actual brand shares were plotted, it was found that the correlation was very close, except in three specific two-month periods. These corresponded to those times when Titan had carried out major national promotions, causing Delta to lose between 1 and 2 per cent of its brand share.

Once those promotional effects had been extracted, 97 per cent of Delta's variation in share of the branded market had been explained. The analysis showed that its base market share was around 10 per cent, and that price changes could increase its share by up to 2 per cent in a two-month period. When it was advertised heavily, its share had increased by no less than 7 per cent. In other words, Delta was particularly sensitive to advertising pressure, and the policy to cut advertising at the end of 1971 had been an error. Management had asked whether they should restore Delta's advertising, and if so to what level. The analysis provided an early answer to this question.

Figure 7.2 shows the effects of price and advertising on Delta's share, and the relationship between the advertising expenditure, measured on a four-month basis, and market share gain. This is another example of a response curve, and it illustrates the law of diminishing returns, for advertising expenditure above £60,000 has little additional effect.

So far, the analysis had explained Delta's share. It was decided that it was more sensible to look at Titan's share next rather than Beta's, because of the initial lack of success when attempting to explain Beta's behaviour in total market terms.

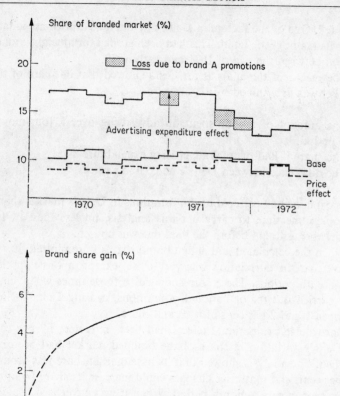

FIGURE 7.2. Effects of price and advertising on Delta's share.

TITAN'S SHARE

At the end of 1969 Titan controlled 33 per cent of the branded market, and by the end of 1972 this had risen to 45 per cent. Over the same period sterling distribution had increased from 50 per cent to nearly 70 per cent. It was known that Titan's sales force had been particularly active over this period, and this had been a major factor in obtaining the increase in distribution. It was logical, therefore, to explain the basic growth in Titan's share in distribution terms. On an annual basis it was found that a 2 per cent increase in the sterling distribution gave a 1·1 per cent increase in share.

This distribution effect was taken out of Titan's share trend, and the residual market share was then analysed, against the following factors:

Titan's price advantage over the average price of Beta and Delta
Titan's advertising expenditure (on a four-month basis)
Titan's share of total advertising expenditure (also on a four-month basis)
Promotional gains and losses.

The analysis consumed a considerable amount of time, and no less than thirty models were considered before the final conclusions were reached. The search for realistic and meaningful relationships is often very frustrating, but useful results can be found if the model-builder is prepared to persevere. (As in all research work, a key asset for the researcher is a 'nose' for knowing when to go on and when to stop.)

In all, 89 per cent of the variations in Titan's share were explained without taking promotions into account, and they increased the percentage to 94. The exact relationship derived was too complicated to explain fully in simple terms. It was found that Titan's share was particularly sensitive to its price advantage over the other major products, its growth in distribution, and to its share of advertising expenditure; but less sensitive to the amount spent on advertising.

The actual and 'fitted' brand-share trends for Titan are shown in Figure 7.3, which illustrates the importance of promotions. Over the period of the analysis Titan had run some very successful promotions, which had gained it up to a 3 per cent share in any two-monthly period. The model explained also why Titan's share had begun to level off – in the main owing to greater difficulty in obtaining increased distribution.

THE DRAKE BRAND-SHARE MODEL

A number of lessons had been learned from this detailed analysis, for which more than sixty regression runs had been carried out before the final models were derived. The conclusions were as follows:

1 For Delta, advertising expenditure must be restored to around £150,000 per year as soon as possible

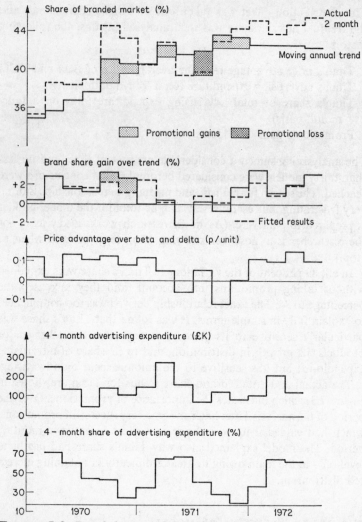

FIGURE 7.3. Brand-share trends for Titan.

2 Delta's price must be maintained at a slightly lower level than that of Titan's

3 Beta's advertising must be increased, so that it is at all times marginally above Titan's

4 In the past Beta's price was nearly always higher than Titan's. Every effort should be made to reverse this trend.

The results of these actions would be

> To return Delta's share, through advertising and price advantage, to around 18 per cent. To reduce Titan's share from 45 per cent to 41 per cent. In turn, this would increase Beta's share from 40 per cent to 41 per cent.

These market-share changes may not sound very spectacular in themselves, but they do represent a reverse in the existing pattern. This marketing policy had other advantages as well. The large increase in advertising expenditure would also reduce 'all-others' total market share, so that the three major brands would have a larger segment of the total market to share among themselves. This alone was worth 2–3 per cent in volume terms.

This policy was followed, and the market shares stabilized around the levels predicted by the model. The complete model is shown in diagram form in Figure 7.4. The boxes on the left-hand side of the diagram show the data that has to be entered into the model, so that the other calculations can follow. It is pertinent to note here that the market-share relationships that have been found will not forecast shares by themselves. They need data based on management judgement about the levels of prices, distribution, and advertising. This type of market-share model can be considered as a set of equations built into a simulation programme, which can then be used by managers to test out a range of alternative plans.

THE LINK BETWEEN PRODUCT AND MARKET MODELS

A number of different models concerned with product planning have been described and, where appropriate, market forecasts have been assumed. The link between market and product models has not yet been mentioned. In practice both types of model tend to be elements in a wider marketing information system.

A market model is a set of mathematical relationships describing the real mechanisms at work in a market and its segments. Normally, these relationships are built into a computer program, which then forms the working tool that a manager can use. The input to the model is data on the market, probably in terms of volume and

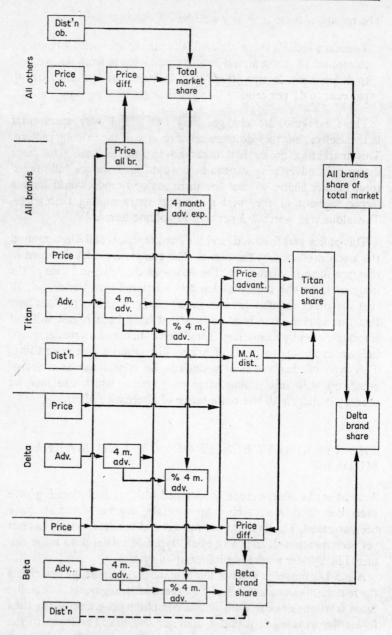

FIGURE 7.4. Drake products brand – share model.

expenditure trends, consumption rates, and so on. This data is structured and stored in a data file on the computer, and is called up automatically by the market model when it is running. The output from the market model is total market forecasts, either in the long or short term, as desired by the manager.

Diagrammatically this arrangement can be represented by three boxes. One box, the data file, feeds into the second box, the market model, which feeds into the third box, the market forecast output. This is shown in the diagram below.

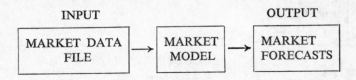

Similarly, for a product model, the input is a data file containing prices, advertising, distribution, etc. for the forecasting period. This feeds into the product model, which incorporates the market-share relationships, such as those described for the Drake Company. The output would be a set of market-share forecasts. This is shown diagrammatically below:

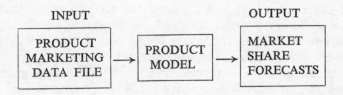

In order to calculate product volumes the market forecasts must also be entered into the market-share model. This link is normally set up by using a third data file, containing the current market forecasts. The data in this file is compiled by the market model whenever the manager decides that a given set of forecasts is the one that he wishes to use for subsequent planning. This data file is therefore set up automatically by the market model, and can then be brought into use by the product model at the appropriate time.

In this way the two linked sets of data file/model/output described previously are joined together by a common data file containing market forecasts. This is shown in the diagram below:

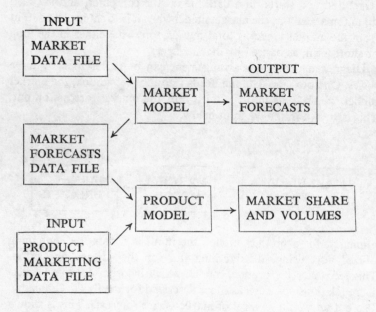

AN EXAMPLE OF THE LINK IN PRACTICE

In Chapter 4 a market model for health products was described. In addition to the market analysis, a detailed evaluation was carried out into the company's products in that market, and various relationships were derived. For these products market-share equations were developed for each pack, by each of three outlets, giving a total of nine market-share equations. When running the market-share model, the manager is able to consider the price and distribution policy he wishes to follow, for each of the product variants, in each of the outlet types. This system went into much greater detail than the Drake Company example, since the managers concerned wished to work at this level in order to gain and maintain control over their market.

A typical output from this market-share model is shown in Figure 7.5. The shares of the market predicted for the brand are listed by pack, and converted into volumes in both units and cases. The manager uses the market-share model to test a number of alternative plans. Having decided on one plan, the particular set of market

```
SHORT (2 YR) OR LONG (5 YR) TERM ? SHORT

STARTING YEAR ? 73

ARE YOU USING 'PLAN' OR 'SIM'ULATION DATA ?
       ANSWER=PLAN

------------------------------------------------------------------------

HEALTH PRODUCT BRAND SHARE MODEL                          16/7/73

SHORT TERM PRODUCT SALES MODEL
========================================================================
```

	QR1	QR2	1974 QR3	QR4	1974 TOTAL	1975 TOTAL
BRAND SHARES						
(OF TOTAL SOLIDS)						
SOLIDS PACK A	30.1	25.9	30.7	32.9	29.7	30.3
SOLIDS PACK B	26.4	23.9	26.9	27.8	26.1	27.9
TOTAL SOLIDS	56.5	49.8	57.6	60.7	55.8	58.2
(OF TOTAL LIQUIDS)						
LIQUID PACK	19.5	13.3	16.9	17.1	16.2	17.0

```
========================================================================
```

SALES (MILL PACKS)	QR1	QR2	QR3	QR4	1974 TOTAL	1975 TOTAL
SOLIDS PACK A	3.439	3.384	3.714	3.728	14.264	14.913
SOLIDS PACK B	3.163	2.936	3.179	3.413	12.692	13.876
TOTAL SOLIDS	6.602	6.320	6.892	7.141	26.956	28.789
LIQUID PACK	1.728	1.518	1.635	1.735	6.616	7.314

```
========================================================================
```

SALES (000 CASES)	QR1	QR2	QR3	QR4	1974 TOTAL	1975 TOTAL
SOLIDS PACK A	286.58	281.96	309.47	310.68	1188.69	1242.75
SOLIDS PACK B	527.24	489.40	529.76	568.89	2115.28	2312.60
TOTAL SOLIDS	813.82	771.36	839.23	879.57	3303.98	3555.35
LIQUID PACK	144.01	126.50	136.28	144.56	551.35	609.46

FIGURE 7.5. Health product brand – share model output.

shares is entered into a data file and stored in the computer. This file is automatically picked up by a product financial model, which has its own data file, containing all the various product costs. The financial model is a third link in the chain with the market and product models. A typical output is the product contribution forecast, as shown in Figure 7.6. The structure of the market, product and financial models is shown in Figure 7.7.

PRODUCT FINANCIAL MODEL

2 YEAR COST AND PROFIT PROJECTIONS   16/7/73

	QR1	QR2	1974 QR3	QR4	1974 TOTAL	1975 TOTAL
TOTAL MARKET(MILL.UNITS)						
	19.8	27.1	19.7	20.4	87.0	90.2
BRAND SHARE (%)	42.0	28.9	43.3	43.4	38.6	40.0
VOLUME (MILL.UNITS)	8.3	7.8	8.5	8.9	33.6	36.1
(000 CASES)	957.8	897.9	975.5	1024.1	3855.3	4164.8
SALES	929	866	941	985	3721	4143
% SALES	100	100	100	100	100	100
- LABOUR	15	14	17	17	64	1204
% SALES	2	2	2	2	2	29
- PACKAGING	115	106	115	120	456	0
% SALES	12	12	12	12	12	0
- RAW MATERIALS	134	125	136	143	538	0
% SALES	14	14	14	15	14	0
(TOTAL PRIME COST)	264	245	268	280	1058	1204
% SALES	28	28	28	28	28	29
GROSS MARGIN	665	621	673	705	2663	2939
% SALES	72	72	72	72	72	71
- ADVERTISING	194	166	205	182	747	839
% SALES	21	19	22	18		20
20						
- SELLING & MARKETING (VARIABLE)	40	38	41	43	161	179
% SALES	4	4	4	4	4	4
- SELLING & MARKETING (FIXED)	39	38	38	38	153	165
% SALES	4	4	4	4	4	4
PRODUCT CONTRIBUTION	392	379	389	442	1602	1756
% SALES	42	44	41	45	43	42

ALL MONEY IN THOUSANDS OF POUNDS. UNITS ARE PACKS

COST FILE IS DATED F73/74

FIGURE 7.6. Health product financial model output.

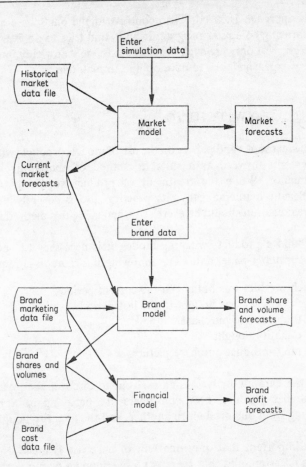

FIGURE 7.7. Health product – model-based marketing information system.

The market, product and financial models are independent of each other, but are linked together by data files. In this way each model is constructed as its particular part of the analysis is completed, and the manager has the use of a working system in the minimum possible time. Each of the programmes is self-contained, and can be more easily developed on the computer. Equally important, it can be modified and improved as time goes on, and adapted to changing management requirements.

This approach is in complete contrast to the one where a large all-embracing computer program is built, and tries to do everything in one go. Not only are such programs extremely unwieldy, but they are very expensive both to develop and to maintain.

PRODUCT SWITCHING

In some textbooks and papers on the use of models product switching is often put forward as a suitable method of analysing product performance. While the treatment of product switching can be very elegant mathematically, its practical use is severely limited, and great caution should be exercised when using this method in real life.

To build a product switching model, it is necessary to have detailed consumer-panel data. The following information is required:

Which product was bought in the current period
Which product was bought in the last period
The frequency of purchase
The quantity bought
The multi-product purchase picture.

From the data an analysis is carried out to discover the loyalty to a particular product, how consumers are behaving in terms of switching from one product to another, and the quantity bought per buyer.

It is important that only one unit of purchase is made on each buying occasion, and that there is no overlapping or multi-product purchase at this time. If these conditions are not met, product-switching analysis cannot be carried out satisfactorily.

Consider a market in which there are three products, and purchasing behaviour is available over three time periods. In period one the shares held by the three products were 45, 30 and 25 per cent respectively. In period two the shares changed to 45, 28 and 27 per cent. As shown in Figure 7.8, buyers have switched from one product to another. For example, of the 45 per cent who bought product 'A' in period one, 36 per cent have remained loyal, 5 per cent have switched to 'B' and 4 per cent to 'C'. A similar pattern emerged between periods two and three.

EXAMPLE: – A consumer product
　　　　 – One 'unit' purchased each time
　　　　 – No multi-brand purchase

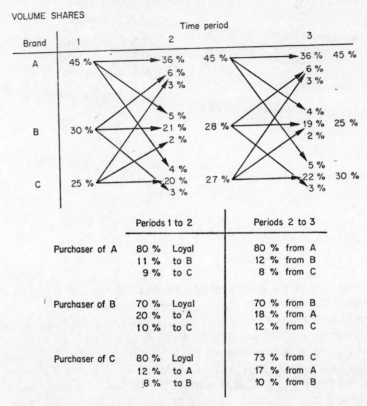

VOLUME SHARES

FIGURE 7.8. Product-switching pattern.

From this data it is possible to draw up a matrix in which the product bought in the last period is represented by the columns and the product bought in this period is represented by rows. Figure 7.9 shows such a matrix for the set of data described above.

Equations can be built up from the matrix to reflect the patterns in the product switching. By changing one of the parameters, say the percentage remaining loyal to 'A', the effects on share can be calculated for succeeding time periods. Assuming starting shares are 45, 30 and 25 per cent for 'A', 'B' and 'C' respectively, and assuming

Assumes: Brand purchased last period
influences current purchase

Brand purchased last period

		A	B	C
Brand purchased this period	A	80 %	12 %	8 %
	B	18 %	70 %	12 %
	C	17 %	10 %	73 %

In general:

		A	B	C
	A	P_{AA}	P_{AB}	P_{AC}
	B	P_{BA}	P_{BB}	P_{BC}
	C	P_{CA}	P_{CB}	P_{CC}

$\Sigma P_{ij} = 1$ for $j = A, B, C$ for any I

FIGURE 7.9. Product-switching matrix.

80 per cent of the buyers remain loyal to 'A', then after six time periods 'A's' share would have dropped to about 44 per cent, 'C's' would have risen to 31 per cent and 'B's' fallen to 25 per cent. After this the share trends are almost stable.

If, however, 85 per cent of the buyers remain loyal to 'A', its share will in fact increase from 45 to 50 per cent within the next six time periods. 'C's' share will not rise as fast as in the previous case and will only reach about 28 per cent but 'B's' will fall faster, and level off at 21 per cent.

By assuming that the switching matrix holds true, you may make simple runs of this nature. These can give an insight into underlying strengths and weaknesses in basic product-share behaviour, but they do not in any way explain real cause and effect relationships between the product share and parameters under the marketing managers' direct control, such as advertising and pricing. Therefore, bearing in mind the limitations that are necessary in order to use product switching, and the consequent limitations on the results that can be obtained, remember that it has not been found to be particularly useful for modelling in practice.

This re-emphasizes the point that all useful models must be based on an analysis of management processes, combined with analysis of the situation management is in. The product models described in this chapter are all based on real work that has been carried out. Each case is different and brings its own problems. It is unlikely that a 'standard' model or even a standard approach will be successful. What is needed is creative teamwork by the manager and the model-builder, each applying his talents in an imaginative way.

8. New-Product Models

The long-term future of any company depends on innovation – on finding ideas for developing, producing and marketing new products. There is a much greater risk of failure, though a greater profit potential, with new than existing products, and the sensitivity of this area of company operations has led to many attempts to model the former. Unfortunately most of the models have been even less successful than the new products they have tried to simulate!

It is not intended to review all the work that has been carried out on new-product models. Most of it falls into the category of a model-builder trying to build the all-purpose model for any new product that will earn him, and the company he works for, the theoretical pot of gold at the end of the rainbow. The major failing of all-purpose models is that they have not really been built to meet a specific need of a practising manager, but rather a general need of many managers. Consequently they have often failed to satisfy any manager!

Nevertheless, there is no doubt about the importance of new products. For example, in many companies an examination of the current product range will show that many of the products did not exist some ten years ago. Much has been written also about increasing rate of change and its tendency to reduce the profitable life of any product. To help plan and control new product activity, management would like an accurate crystal ball. As yet, this does not exist, but the imaginative use of models can be a step in that direction.

THE STAGES OF NEW-PRODUCT DEVELOPMENT

In order to examine the use of models in new-product evaluation and planning, it is useful to split the progress of a new product from initial conception to full production into a number of steps. Models have been used to aid planning at the various stages, each model being independent of those in other stages. Again, a modular approach is preferable. During new-product development, management's major decision is whether the product should proceed to the next stage in the development cycle. The objective of the model-builder is to produce a model that will help the manager in this decision, particularly by introducing a higher degree of objectivity into what is often an emotional area. Some stages in new product development will now be examined and the use of models described. This is followed by the description of two working systems, as examples.

STAGE 1 THE SEARCH

In this stage all new ideas are analysed, with the objective of deciding whether any one of them contains a germ of success. Market models can be useful in this area, assuming that the company has sufficient data to make a detailed examination of the market worth while. The market models described in Chapter 3 were for existing products, but they can also identify areas of growth where new-product innovation should be possible.

One technique that has been used to find gaps in markets for new products is 'cluster analysis', in which existing products are linked together by common economic and marketing characteristics, so that any gaps between the clusters are revealed. It is necessary to have a considerable amount of detailed data on the market to carry this out. This necessity has tended to limit the use of cluster analysis to companies that are already in a market, and are looking for new products to extend their existing range.

Simulation models can also be used to aid searching, particularly where market data is available and the manager wishes to test his judgement on, say, the size of potential markets. The response function approach can be used just as well for markets in this situation, although, when they were described earlier, only product cases were examined.

Where the search is aimed at deciding which of several markets should be attacked next, risk analysis has been used. The likely return from each course of action is examined for each of the markets, and the model indicates the market that gives the best return. The models incorporate probability calculations and often use discounted-cash-flow methods of evaluation. The output from the model is a valuable input to the decision-making processes.

To summarize, models are used to aid managers in the search phase, and help them to decide which markets and/or which new products to take to the next stage.

STAGE 2 SCREENING

Screening may be defined as an analysis of the chosen idea against a framework of company experience, such as a screening grid. The following were typical factors considered in the screening of one product:

(a) *Total market* – current size, historical growth patterns, long-term prospects, economic sensitivity, demographic profiles, regional profiles, seasonality
(b) *Competition* – companies and brands in the market, marketing expenditure levels, prices, trade margins
(c) *The product* – product differentiation, company image, brand image, product technology
(d) *Selling and distribution* – sales force, outlet types, distribution methods.

In our experience models have not been used directly in screening, but an assessment of each of the factors involved is important, so that the manager can answer the question 'Does the product reach the minimum standards required, and does it fit in with the patterns that the company has established?' If the screening criteria are satisfied, then the product can enter the third stage.

STAGE 3 EVALUATION

At this stage the manager makes a detailed marketing, financial and production analysis on all aspects of the proposed product. The objective is to decide whether the product should be developed further. Models, particularly simulation models, have proven very useful.

STAGE 4 DEVELOPMENT

This stage is the one in which money is really committed to the development of the product. Expenditure is incurred on design and development, and considerable management time is devoted to comprehensive planning for production, marketing, selling and distribution. At the end of this stage the final decision to 'go' for production is taken. A model developed for use in evaluation can be used also during the development stage. Timing now becomes important, because, as time marches on, more money is committed to the new product. Therefore the simulation model sometimes incorporates a form of network analysis (e.g. PERT), for the control of the development and launch phases.

STAGE 5 TESTING

For consumer products this is the stage when the product will be launched into a test market, so that consumer reaction can be measured. For engineering products testing is carried out with production prototypes. During the testing stage the build-up to full production takes place. The objective of this stage is to confirm the decision to launch the product.

For consumer products models are being used to help monitor test markets and particularly to evaluate their results. Such models rely not only on the market research data collected from the regions where the test market is being held but also on a detailed analysis of ex-factory sales data. The monitoring is often helped by the collection of special data by the sales force in the test regions.

CASE STUDY – A MODEL FOR NEW PRODUCT EVALUATION AND DEVELOPMENT

The first example was originally developed for a tobacco company, where new-products introduction was a continuing part of the general marketing activity. Management decided to use a model in an attempt to examine, in more detail, the risk involved in new-product launches.

MANAGEMENT SPECIFICATION

Before construction began, a thorough analysis of the new-product planning procedure was carried out, as usual, in terms of objectives, tasks and processes. As a result it was decided to build the model to simulate the marketing and financial plans, so that a product's sensitivity to variations in assumptions on volumes and costs could be evaluated rapidly. Such an evaluation was the main factor in the management's specification of requirements.

DATA USED

The following data was collected for each new product:

1 Forecasts of the total market and the segment into which the product was to be launched
2 The target market share
3 The marketing costs involved (advertising and promotions)
4 Product selling price
5 The costs of tobacco and tobacco duty
6 Wages and packaging costs
7 Certain production costs
8 Fixed cost of plant and machinery that needed to be bought in order to make the new product
9 Stock levels for tobacco, packaging, finished goods and work-in-progress
10 The cost of debtors
11 An investment grant (if appropriate).

A structured set of data was built up for each product for five years ahead from the launch date, and was entered into the system. The data bank was set up on a time-sharing computer, wherein each product was identified separately.

MODES OF OPERATION

The model had two main methods of operation. The first was an 'input' mode, which was used when data was entered for the first time. This made sure that all the data was entered correctly, and that sufficient data was available to enable a financial evaluation to be

```
NEW BRAND NUMBER  500(11)                    OUTPUT DATE 11/8/70

                                             TARGET SHARE 10 %
LAUNCH DATE 1/9/72                    LAUNCH DURATION = 18 MONTHS
CURRENCY - 000 POUNDS. VOLUMES - MILLION
----------------------------------------------------------------


CLASSIFICATION          =1         SUBSTITUTION    = 0 %
TOBACCO STOCK           =24 MONTHS  PACKAGING STOCK = 8 WEEKS
FIN.GOODS + W.I.P STOCK =8 WEEKS    COST OF DEBTORS = 12 %
INVESTMENT GRANT        = 40 %
```

YEAR	1972	1973	1974	1975	1976	1977
BRAND SHARE FORECAST (%)						
EXPECTED	4.1	8.9	10.0	10.0	10.0	10.0
LOWER	3.3	5.0	4.6	4.4	4.2	4.0
FAILURE	2.5	3.2	3.0	2.9	2.7	2.6
BRAND VOLUME FORECASTS (MILLIONS)						
EXPECTED	10.948	58.252	68.145	70.000	72.000	73.000
LOWER	8.758	32.372	31.583	30.809	30.104	29.997
FAILURE	6.569	20.975	20.463	19.962	19.506	18.788
VARIABLE COSTS (POUNDS/100)						
NET SELLING PRICE	4.33	4.33	4.53	4.73	4.73	4.93
TOBACCO COST	.52	.52	.52	.54	.56	.58
TOBACCO DUTY	2.14	2.34	2.34	2.49	2.49	2.49
WAGES COST	.36	.37	.40	.42	.45	.47
PACKAGING COST	.10	.10	.11	.11	.12	.12
MODEL PARTS	.273	.273	.261	.252	.248	.248
FIXED COSTS (000 POUNDS)						
MARKETING	170	200	210	220	235	250
PLANT AND MACHINES	100	50	0	0	50	0
OUTPUT PER MACHINE	1.10	1.10	1.15	1.19	1.21	1.21

FIGURE 8.1. A new-product model – data listing.

carried out. The second mode of operation used data that had either just been entered or was available from the data file, to carry out a straightforward simulation. A typical print-out to list the data stored on file is shown in Figure 8.1. In this example the product was due to be launched on 1 September 1972 and the marketing manager had set a target share of 10 per cent to be reached 18 months after launch. On this print-out there is a brand-share forecast that has been generated by a separate sub-model within the evaluation system.

BRAND-SHARE SUB-MODEL

To build the brand-share sub-model, an analysis was first made of previous new-product launches over recent years. This gave empirical brand-share growth pattern, which could generate a growth curve to meet a given target market share, in any given time. For example, if a manager wished to simulate the effects of obtaining 10 per cent of the market in 18 months, the appropriate curve would be generated.

In addition, it was decided by management that two other situations should be examined automatically. The first was set at a lower level of success, defined as the brand-share trend that reached half the original target. The second was a failure level, where the product reached only a third of the target before levelling off.

The use of these models to generate brand-share forecasts enabled alternative brand-share and time targets to be evaluated in a simple manner. The masses of detailed calculations that could follow from

```
NEW BRAND NUMBER 500(11)                        OUTPUT DATE  6/8/70

LAUNCH DATE     1/9/72                          TARGET SHARE = 10 %
                                         LAUNCH DURATION = 18 MONTHS
CURRENCY - 000 POUNDS. VOLUMES - MILLION
------------------------------------------------------------------

BRAND SHARE ACCUMULATION DURING LAUNCH

      0.0%                    5.0%                    10.0%

MONTHS
------------------------------------------------------------------
 1    )    *.+
 2    )      *  . +
 3    )        *.   .   +
 4    )          *  .      +
 5    )          *    .      +
 6    )          *      .      +
 7    )          *        .      +
 8    )          *          .      +
 9    )          *            .      +
10    )          *             .      +
11    )          *             .      +
12    )          *             .      +
13    )          *            .      +
14    )          *           .      +
15    )          *          .      +
16    )          *         .      +
17    )          *        .      +
18    )          *       .      +
..................*......*....................*...................
19    )          *     .      +
20    )          *    .      +
21    )          *   .      +
22    )          *  .      +
23    )          *  .      +
24    )          *  .      +
25    )          *  .      +
26    )          *  .      +
27    )          *  .      +
```

FIGURE 8.2. A new-product model – normal, lower and failure level brand-share forecasts.

a decision to change from 10 per cent in 18 months to, say, 8 per cent in 20 months, with the launch put back two months, could be carried out with ease. A typical print-out of the brand-share picture is shown in Figure 8.2. The brand share from this graph was then related to the total market volume forecasts, which also included seasonal factors, and new product volume calculations were then made.

FINANCIAL CALCULATIONS

Once the marketing volumes had been established, the evaluation model was able to carry out normal contribution calculations, based on those volumes, taking into account the prices and costs specified in the data file. These calculations were normally made for the launch year and the following five years. A typical output is shown in Figure 8.3, where the contribution is negative for 1972 but positive from 1973 onwards. This plan assumes that the target share of 10 per cent is met within 18 months of launch. The second half of this output is concerned with the contribution that is made if the product reaches either the lower or the failure level of brand share.

In addition to the contribution calculations, a further print-out could be obtained. This examined the investment required in stocks, debtors and in equipment, so that a return on investment could be calculated.

The third output is the cash flow associated with the new-product launch. An example is shown in Figure 8.4, where the net cash flow does not become positive until nearly two years after launch. When this output was obtained, a discount rate of 16·5 per cent was considered reasonable. If the product reached its target share, the net present value at that rate is positive. Suffice to say that, for both the lower and failure levels, the net present value of the cash flow is negative at the target discount rate.

The basic set of calculations within this model was designed to be applicable to any new product launched by the tobacco company. It included the calculations normally made in the budgeting procedure. The brand-share sub-model was based on analysis of previous new products, and, as it was specifically designed to meet certain management needs, it would probably not be useful to other companies.

```
NEW BRAND NUMBER 500(11)                        OUTPUT DATE 6/8/70
                                      TARGET SHARE = 10 %
LAUNCH DATE 1/9/72                    LAUNCH DURATION = 18 MONTHS
CURRENCY - 000 POUNDS.   VOLUMES - MILLION
-------------------------------------------------------------------
```

	1972	1973	1974	1975	1976	1977
VOLUME	11	58	68	70	72	73
NET SALES VALUE	474	2522	3087	3311	3406	3599
TOBACCO COST	57	303	354	378	403	427
TOBACCO DUTY	234	1363	1595	1743	1793	1818
WAGES COST	39	216	273	294	324	343
PACKAGING COST	11	58	75	77	86	88
TOTAL VARIABLE COST	342	1940	2296	2492	2606	2672
GROSS PROFIT	132	583	790	819	799	927
MARKETING	170	200	210	220	235	250
CONTRIBUTION	-38	383	580	599	564	677
LOWER LEVE						
VOLUME	9	32	32	31	30	29
NET SALES VALUE	379	1402	1431	1457	1424	1430
GROSS PROFIT	106	324	366	360	334	368
CONTRIBUTION	-64	124	156	140	99	118
FAILURE LEVEL						
VOLUME	7	21	20	20	20	19
NET SALES VALUE	284	908	927	944	923	926
GROSS PROFIT	79	210	237	234	217	239
CONTRIBUTION	-91	10	27	14	-18	-11

FIGURE 8.3. A new-product model – contribution forecasts.

USE OF THE MODEL

The model was used to check out many new products. A series of data files on each product was built up, so that continuous evaluation could be made over the period up to, and including, launch. Using the model on a regular basis gave rise to a system of management control that allowed all the products to be evaluated on a consistent and more objective basis.

```
NEW BRAND NUMBER 500(11)                        OUTPUT DATE 6/8/70

                                            TARGET SHARE = 10 %
LAUNCH DATE 1/9/72                     LAUNCH DURATION = 18 MONTHS
CURRENCY - 000 POUNDS, VOLUMES - MILLION
------------------------------------------------------------------
```

INVESTMENT AT YEAR END	1972	1973	1974	1975	1976	1977
IN STOCKS AND DEBTORS						
TOBACCO	657	718	738	783	783	783
PACKAGING	7	9	12	12	13	13
FINISHED GOODS	64	89	108	115	125	131
DEBTORS	57	303	370	397	409	432
TOTAL STOCKS + DEBTORS	785	1119	1228	1307	1330	1360
IN EQUIPMENT						
MODEL PARTS	30	159	180	180	183	186
PLANT AND MACHINES	100	150	150	150	200	200
INVESTMENT GRANT	0	52	72	8	0	21
NET INV. IN EQUIPMENT	130	257	58	322	383	365
NET INVESTMENT	915	1376	1487	1629	1713	1725
RETURN ON INVESTMENT (%)						
LOWER	-7	17	21	18	12	14
EXPECTED	-4	28	39	37	33	39
FAILURE	-11	2	5	2	-3	-2

FIGURE 8.4. A new-product model – cash flow forecast.

Similar models have been used in other companies. The most interesting was one that discovered, to many managers' surprise, that the company concerned had no less than sixty products 'in the pipeline'. When these had been evaluated, using the model, only twenty remained, and some of these failed to make it into production!

TIMING ASPECTS

Timing is a critical factor when considering new-product development. If the initial launch dates slip, or are delayed by elements outside the company's control, the projected financial performance of the new product may have to be reappraised. It has been found useful to associate the financial simulation model with a model of the timing aspects, expressed as a network. On most time-sharing computers there are very powerful network packages, which can be used as a sub-routine to the financial model.

Analysis of the new-product decision processes must be made, in order to specify the network and to decide which events should be included in the system. If the system is to be used for more than one new product, a standard network will probably be required. Using this method, those events that do not apply for a particular product can be cut out by giving them zero duration.

In the tobacco company a simple network model was set up. The relevant dates were entered at the same time as other data on the new product, and these dates were stored in the data file. Once the product was on the system, its progress could be controlled by using the network every time a new simulation was made. In this way a close check was kept on the product's progress during the development phase.

Any change to the dates could immediately be reflected in the financial performance of the product, by using the simulation model. In this way the two parts of the model were closely linked.

PROGRESSIVE EVALUATION

With the passage of time more data on a market or a product becomes available. This is entered into the data file at a suitable time and is evaluated by using the model. In the tobacco model regular monitoring was carried out for every product in the system, on a monthly basis.

The management use of the simulation model was concerned with examining alternative policies, with balancing the profit against the investment required, and with considering all potential rewards against the risks involved. Only by carrying out this evaluation in detail, at each step of the new-product development, can risks associated with a new-product launch be reduced.

The financial, marketing and timing models were used right up to the product launch. At all stages the management decisions taken were based on the data that had been carefully collected, analysed and evaluated. The models provided managers with an extremely flexible and important tool that coordinated all aspects of new-product activity.

CASE STUDY – A NEW-PRODUCT CASH FLOW MODEL

The second example of a model to assist new-product planning was that used in a company where it had been found extremely difficult to build deterministic models for producing new-product sales forecasts. In the model management judgement was used as the main basis of calculating a 'sales profile'.

MANAGEMENT SPECIFICATION

The main objective of the model was to compare the likely sales rate with production capacity. If a capacity shortfall became apparent, then further investment for the product could be evaluated, and the effects on cash flow determined. The major output of the model was a five-year cash flow, taking into account contribution from the product, investment and all product costs.

SALES ESTIMATES

The manager stated the way in which he estimated sales would grow and settle down in the test market. At this stage no assumptions were made about either the size or the location of the test area.

An index of 100 was defined as the level at which the product would settle down after two years in the test market. The manager gave relevant index levels for the previous eight quarters. This gave the facility to examine any sales profile. For example, if the manager wished to consider an earlier settling down level, he made the appropriate input.

TEST AREAS

Once the sales profile had been described, the next stage was to relate the test areas together. The following data was required:

1 The number of sales areas (any number could be used)

2 The relative market sizes of these areas (e.g. population, or the company's current sales in these areas)
3 A code number for each test area
4 The order and timing of successive launches of the product into further areas, before it was launched nationally.

The model took all the data and used it to calculate the sales of the product in each area, by quarter. A total sales profile was built up, covering both test market and national launch.

SALES V CAPACITY BALANCE

Next, further details on the product were entered into the model. These included price, production costs, number of units per case, planned production capacity, product shelf life, and stock-in-hand at the start of launch. Using the sales profile, calculations were made to compare the sales rate against stock and production capacity. If there was a production shortfall, the manager had to decide whether he should allocate extra capacity to this product. If he did so, the cost for this was taken into account. The data on the product also included trade margins and gross contribution rates for the product. This enabled the computer to calculate the contribution in cash flow terms.

USE OF MODEL

The objective of this model was to test the sensitivity of the cash flow to changes in market volume, test market, pricing, or capacity constraints. It was a pure simulation model, built up very simply. It was particularly useful in helping managers to decide in which test markets they would launch their products, at what rate, and if they were successful, when they would go national.

This type of model can easily be linked to the type of model described for the tobacco company. It is a further example of the assembly of modules to form more complex systems.

SYSTEM-DEVELOPMENT PROGRAMME

Models used in new product activity are not normally considered in isolation from other models. In a way similar to the linking of market and product models through the use of common data files, new-product models may be linked also into a common system. The need for a system-development programme was emphasized in Chapter 2. The place of new-product models needs to be identified in this programme.

New-product models have generally been developed in companies later than models used for existing products. They are often linked with models of markets that were constructed for other products. The knowledge built up during the analysis stage with the market and product models enables ideas to be generated on the best form of the models to be used with new products. If a company's first modelling activity were in the new-product area, it would probably be quite difficult to build a really useful management tool.

9. *A Five-Year Planning Model*

INTRODUCTION

The U.K. division of a large international chemical group manufactures and distributes a wide range of products, in one well-defined sector of the toiletries market in the U.K., where it is the major force. In 1971 the managing director of the division, a firm believer in planning, decided that the time had come to do something about the division's planning processes. He regarded the existing planning procedure as a 'meaningless ritual', sometimes referring to it as 'the annual square dance'. (Being an ex-marketing man, he was given to colourful turns of phrase.) Certainly he believed that the planning process between his division and the group headquarters did not allow a 'meaningful planning dialogue' to take place.

His position in the hierarchy did not enable him to do much about international planning, so he decided to do something in his own division, in the hope that a shining example would lead to general improvements. Informally he created a consensus of opinion that both supported this approach and his intention to use consultants. He had formed this intention because his own staff did not have the capacity to undertake the work, because he needed an objective view of the situation, and because he suspected his division did not have all the technical skills he thought would be required.

He selected a consulting firm, briefed and interviewed them, investigated their track record, and asked them to carry out a survey.

THE SURVEY

The terms of reference for the survey were debated at length. They may be summarized as follows:

1 To examine the processes used in the division to produce the five-year plan

2 To comment on these processes and to say how they could be improved
3 To recommend a programme of work consisting of a number of phases. For each phase to say:
    What would be accomplished
    How it would be of benefit
    What it would cost
    How long it would take.

The survey was followed by a presentation of the assignment proposals to a meeting of senior managers. After discussion, approval was given, and the assignment started.

THE ANALYSIS PHASE

Two consultants were assigned to the job. Both were experienced planning-system designers, with extensive modelling experience, and both had been line managers. One was an economist by training and the other was an engineer.

At the discussion during the presentation of the survey results, a number of salient points had emerged regarding management's objectives for the system:

1 There was to be no empire-building. The division did not need a large planning staff
2 Planning was, and was to remain, one of the jobs of line managers, with some assistance from the three men in the management services
3 The system was to be as simple as possible. Paperwork was to be kept to a minimum. The amount of time managers spent on planning was too much now, and had to be reduced. 'We shall soon be spending all our time planning, and no time doing!'
4 In reply to a question to the managing director: 'No, I have no objection to the use of computers, but it seems to me that that's more likely to slow us down than speed us up.'
5 'Most important, the planning has got to mean something. It's got to be relevant to what we are doing, and intend to do. It's not got to be just a load of figures put together by some accountant.'

6 Lastly, 'It's got to work when you have gone. You must ensure that we understand the system, and can take it on ourselves and develop it.'

The situation was not unfamiliar to the consultants. They suspected, rightly as it turned out, that 'meaningful planning' would involve a penetrating look at a very complex process. They suspected also that no one man in the division would know everything about the existing planning process. 'It's a Topsy system', said one consultant. 'It's just growed'. 'Let's find the man who knows most about Topsy', said the other.

IDENTIFICATION OF PROCESSES

This man was the head of the management services group. He knew most about the system simply because he had the responsibility for producing the final planning document. To do this, he had to pilot it around the various departments concerned. He was involved with production, purchasing, costing, accounting, marketing, distribution and selling. In addition, he had responsibility for market research, data analysis, and anything even vaguely quantitative that no-one else would do. He was fairly busy.

He was thirty-five years old and had been with the division all his working life. He was numerate, systematically minded, and able to make a clear distinction between tasks and processes, although he was involved with both.

'Let's start from the end', said the consultants. 'Let's take your present five-year plan and work backwards, and you can explain how you got there.'

The 'end' was a document that consisted of a descriptive section setting out what the division intended to do in the next five years (called the 'scenario' – someone had read Ackoff), and a quantitative section that expressed those intentions in accounting terms. For each of the five years return on assets and group net profit in millions of pounds was predicted, so that the final output of the planning process, after manipulation of thousands of numbers, was two rows of figures that looked like this:

	1971	1972	1973	1974	1975
Return on assets (%)	8·9	12·3	9·4	10·3	8·7
Group net profit (£M)	4·1	6·2	4·7	5·5	5·8

DEFINING THE LOGIC OF THE MODEL

It took eight weeks of relentless detective work by the management services manager and the consultants before the logic of the processes leading to the production of these figures was identified and recorded. The problem was not the complexity of the processes themselves, although they were complex, but the fact that they were carried out by a number of managers acting in sequence, each aware only of his part in the process. It was not surprising that illogicalities and gaps were discovered. These were resolved in group discussions, and a planning logic that would be the basis for the model was produced. This is shown in simplified form in Figure 9.1, and can best be described by reference to that figure.

During the investigation period, the idea of building a model of the planning process had been gently sold to the managers concerned with planning, first as a means of investigation and analysis, and second as the possible basis for a working system. The virtues of using a terminal, to hold a planning dialogue with a computer, had been extolled. Demonstrations of a simple planning model in use had taken place.

Figure 9.1, suitably extended to deal with the real planning needs of the managers, was the way in which the system was described. The consultant said, 'Imagine I am the computer. Let's go through the processes of producing a corporate plan. We won't be concerned with the numbers yet, but only with our thought processes, and how our decisions have to be structured and made. It's essential that all of us agree that this is a good way to plan what we want to happen to the division, before we start putting it on to a computer. We think it's good enough, but we can easily change or extend bits, if you want it done differently.

'We start at the top of the diagram (Figure 9.1). We know a great deal about consumer and manufacturers' behaviour, as a result of the analysis we have carried out, and the managers will have this in mind when they carry out their planning. There is a fair amount of judgement going into the planning at this stage. There always will be.

'The key to our performance over the next five years, leaving investment aside for the moment, lies in the relative movement of costs, prices and volumes. You know how complicated it is to work

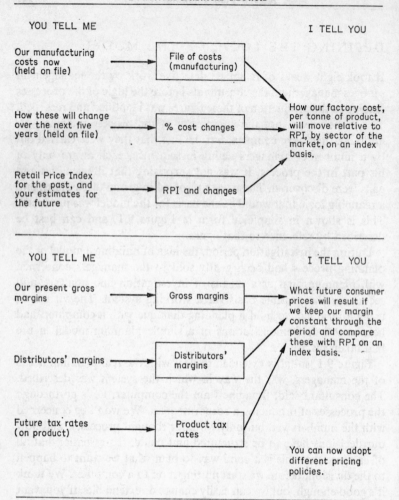

FIGURE 9.1a. The logic of the planning process (assume the computer is speaking).

material price changes through to product cost changes. You know how wide our product range is in each market sector.

'For this reason, we start with a file of manufacturing costs, which cover raw materials, wages, packing and factory overheads. We also include product specifications. We also need to know how we expect these to change over the next five years, and to put these

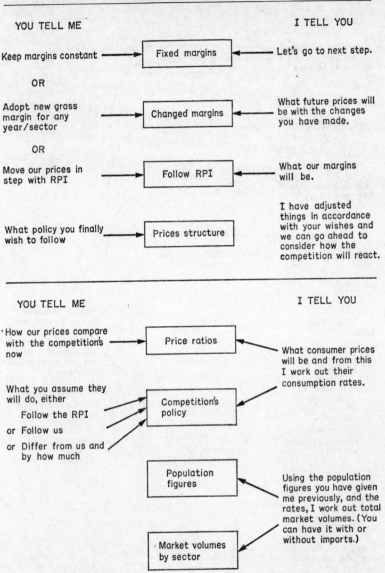

FIGURE 9.1b.

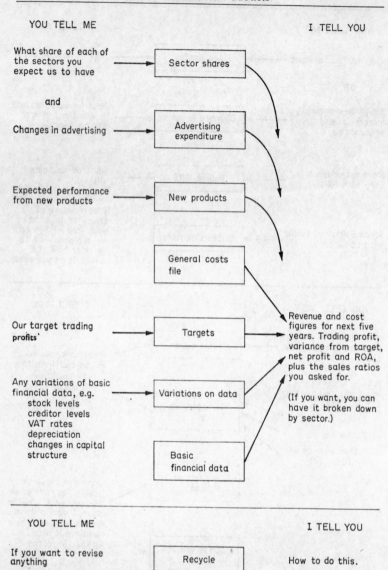

FIGURE 9.1c.

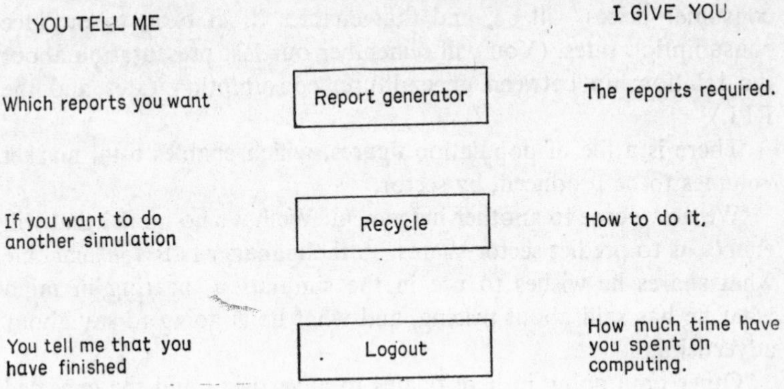

YOU TELL ME   I GIVE YOU

Which reports you want | Report generator | The reports required.

If you want to do
another simulation | Recycle | How to do it.

You tell me that you   How much time have
have finished | . Logout | you spent on
                                                              computing.

FIGURE 9.1d.

expectations into another file. (We can edit these files to change any figures we want to.)

'The first thing we do then is to use the computer to work out how our manufacturing costs, expressed as factory cost per ton of product in each sector, will move relative to inflation (Retail Price Index, see Figure 9.1).

'We now move on to the way we can work out the effects of our pricing policies. The first thing we do is to tell the computer what our present gross margins are, and what we think distributors' margins and product tax rates will be, assuming we keep our margins constant throughout the period, and compare these, on an index basis, with changes in RPI.

'We can go on from this point without making any changes, or we can adopt new gross margins for any year or sector. A third course open to us is to move our prices in step with the RPI. The computer will then work out the gross margins we should get if we did this. This aspect is becoming increasingly important as the government becomes more involved in pricing policies. We have examined this area in depth with the marketing people, and they agree that the model provides a very flexible approach to examining pricing alternatives. We can go round this part of the loop as many times as we need to.

'Now we go on to consider what the opposition may do. We can assume they will follow our lead, as they usually have in the past, follow the RPI, or differ from us by a given amount.

'The machine now has enough data to work out what the industry consumer prices will be, and that enables it, in turn, to produce consumption rates. (You will remember our last presentation about the relationship between expenditure, consumption rates and the RPI.)

'There is a file of population figures, which enables total market volumes to be produced, by sector.

'We now come to another judgement. We have no model that will enable us to predict sector shares, so the manager tells the machine what shares he wishes to use in the simulation, bearing in mind what he has said about pricing, and what he is going to say about advertising.

'Other data going in here relates to advertising and the expected performance from new products, at an aggregated level.

'All the general costs have been identified and classified with the accounts, and they will be on file.

'Changes to these and target trading profits now go in, and the machine produces a financial analysis broken down by sector if required.

'This is the feedback from the simulation. What it says is that, with these RPIs, with this pricing policy, with those shares of the sectors, we shall perform thus. So we shall be able to try all kinds of assumptions, and combinations of them, in our attempts to produce a robust plan for the company. We go around this loop until we are happy, and then we can get a variety of reports that have been agreed with the accountants. You don't have to have the lot, just what you need.'

There then followed a discussion of five hours, as the various managers questioned and probed the proposals. Minor amendments were made, but, in essence, the proposal was accepted, and later that week programming started using a service provided by a time-sharing company.

Programming took two weeks, after which the training of the managers concerned was begun formally. Up to that time they had been closely involved in the design of the system, and were very keen to try it in practice.

FIRST USE OF THE SYSTEM

The work had been timed so that the system was ready for use six weeks before the five-year plan had to be submitted to the group headquarters. This decision showed a great deal of faith in the proposals, since the time required to produce one plan, with no alternatives considered, using the existing methods, was fifteen weeks.

The management services manager and his assistant were the first people to use the system. They did a number of simulations to learn which terminal buttons to press, and how to use all the facilities provided by the system. They then assembled the managers with planning responsibility from purchasing, production, marketing and finance. After a demonstration, on the terminal, the team started planning work, the assumptions used in each simulation being recorded on a simple form that had been specially designed. Simulations took about an hour on average, depending on the number of cycles carried out in the optional loops.

The results of each simulation were fed back to the team and discussed. This discussion led to new simulations, and the process was repeated as the team 'explored' its way to a good five-year plan. Over the six weeks numerous plans were examined with the aid of the system, and the final document prepared for submission to the group was described as 'a model of precision and well documented alternatives'.

Since the reader cannot have a knowledge of the markets of this division, it is difficult to explain the subtleties of the planning decision-making. Two general examples of the questions examined, however, are given below:

1 The expected movement in price of one of the basic raw materials, which was bought forward, if reflected directly in consumer prices, by maintenance of margins, would cause very good profits to be made in the earlier years but lower (although still good) profits in later years. What pricing policy would produce more stability in profit performance over the planning period?
2 Examination of some sectors showed that costs were rising much more rapidly than the RPI. What were the alternatives as regards pricing in the sectors, and what would be the effects of different competitive response?

MAINTENANCE AND DEVELOPMENT

The maintenance of the system, and its development as requirements changed and management became more skilled in its use, was the responsibility of the management services department, which called the consultants back to help with major extensions. After four years' use the system had changed considerably, having been simplified in some respects and extended in others. The high level of the language used, and the ease with which programmes could be changed on the time-sharing service, made this a simple task.

EFFECT ON THE GROUP PLANNING

The improvement in the quality of its plans and the achievement of a very good profit performance by the division, as had been predicted in the plans, was not lost on the group. The work in the division stimulated a general move in the direction of model-based systems throughout the group, with backing from the central management services, who had up to that time concentrated on more traditional activities.

EFFECT ON THE DIVISION

At the end of the planning cycle, the managing director called a meeting to review the achievements of the project. The following comments were recorded:

'For the first time, we all understand our planning processes. We all argue in the same language.'

'We now do in one hour what used to take fifteen weeks.'

'Because of this, we examine a much wider range of possibilities, and I think we are much more creative in our planning.'

'We can answer questions from Group in a few hours. Mind you, this has made them ask us a lot more!'

'The system has broken down the barrier between accounting, marketing, production and so on. We now operate as a team.'

'If anything unexpected happens, we can quickly work out the effects. I can now change tack more quickly than I could before.'

10. *A Model-Based System for Planning International Investment*

This example of the design, construction and use of a model-based planning system centres around the need for methods to plan investment in plant on a multi-national basis. We are grateful to the management of CPC Europe, for permission to use the material presented in this chapter. It is a précis of the key factors that emerged during the design, construction and early use of their 'Facility Planning System'. The work described took place in 1972 and 1973. At that time, we believe, this was among the most advanced business applications of models and computers in the world.

THE COMPANY – CPC EUROPE

CPC Europe is a group of food companies in twenty countries, producing a wide variety of consumer and industrial products, with 20,000 employees, fifty-five factories, and seven research centres. Its sales in 1973 were $754,000,000. Headquarters are in Brussels.

Its internationally known range of consumer products includes Knorr soups, bouillons, seasonings, sauces and other convenience foods; Maizena kitchen starch; Gerber baby foods; Mazola corn oil; Dextro-Energen tablets; and Alsa desserts. It is also a leading processor of corn (maize), producing more than 500 specialized bulk ingredients, including starches, sweeteners, adhesives and other specialities, for some sixty basic food and non-food industries.

CPC Europe is the largest division of CPC International, a worldwide enterprise with operations in forty-six countries, 43,000 employees, and a 1973 sales volume of $1,800,000,000.

CPC EUROPE'S PLANNING SYSTEM

Over a number of years the headquarters planning staff had designed and implemented a comprehensive planning system, by means of which the planning activity of affiliates, of the headquarters and the dialogue between the two was carried out. By 1971 the system had reached the point where further development was required. The use of computers had become an obvious necessity, for the manual system was reaching its limit, and could not satisfy the real planning needs of the management. There were a number of planning areas to be taken into account.

CONSUMER DIVISION

In this division planning had a strong marketing orientation. There was a difficult task of coordination and consolidation of the marketing plans for a very wide range of products in many European countries.

INDUSTRIAL DIVISION

Here the emphasis in the planning process was more orientated towards allocating demand to capacity. There was a greater production orientation than in the Consumer Division, although here too, the number of products was large.

FINANCIAL PLANNING

Financial planning were concerned with the consolidation of the plans of the two divisions, using normal financial methods, and with overall financial planning.

FACILITY PLANNING

The fourth area of planning, the subject of this chapter, was concerned mainly with investment in plant. Naturally there was a high engineering content in the planning processes. Designing the computer-based system for use by the facility planners brought up problems of a particularly challenging nature. The resulting facility planning system (FPS) provides a very good example of the way in which a manager can use computing power to assist him directly in his planning processes.

THE FACILITY PLANNING SYSTEM

MANAGEMENT OBJECTIVE

This was to establish across the European affiliates a pattern of plant investment that would keep manufacturing capacity in step with predicted demand at minimum investment cost, within certain management guide lines.

THE MANAGEMENT TASK

The objective could be achieved only by a combination of system and operational planning.

1 *System planning task.* To design and install a system for planning and control of plant investment that could be used to achieve the objective, and to keep this system updated.
2 *Operational planning task.* To use the facility planning system on an on-going basis to help determine annual investment programmes for Europe, in conjunction with the other planners in the headquarters. There were very close links between the Facility Planning System and the Industrial Division.

DETERMINING THE PLANNING LOGIC

Consultants were employed to assist in the design tasks. The usual manager-consultant teams were formed, and they recorded and analysed the existing methods of allocating investment funds. The rest of this chapter describes the system that evolved from this base. Understanding the system completely would necessitate a detailed knowledge of the company and its plants, but as it is not possible to give this in one chapter, the system is described in outline only.

AN OVER-VIEW OF THE FPS

The planners use the FPS for three main functions:

1 To translate the market forecasts from the Industrial Division into production terms, so that these may be compared with capacity
2 To generate production expansion alternatives that are practical from an engineering viewpoint
3 To develop the investment plans needed to provide enough capacity to meet forecast demands.

THE PRODUCTION PROCESSES

The industrial production process begins with the processing of corn. This leads to a set of first-order products and semi-finished products. A number of further major manufacturing processes, such as spray drying, refining and modification, then result in a series of second- and third-order products. The analysis of the production process identified seventeen major 'channels' that could be directly related to the problem of plant investment.

The production process included a cascading effect. Enough product had to be produced at any level, in any channel, to satisfy the sales requirements for the product itself and the products produced from it, and also satisfy inter-plant requirements.

All plants did not have the same production facilities. A general process logic was therefore produced and then modified to reflect plant differences.

INVESTMENT PROFILES

The various plants responded in different ways to investment. Increasing capacity in one channel of a plant might imply the need for expansion in another channel higher up in the plant network. An investment profile module, which was designed, provided data about the manner in which each facility, in each plant, could be expanded, and gave the necessary investment costs. The information showed a sequence of step increases in capacity, which had to be carried out in a specified order because of technological considerations, and their associated costs. The latter were further detailed into an investment schedule, which specified, on a quarterly basis, the expenditure profile in relation to the quarter when the extra capacity would come on-stream.

OPERATION OF THE SYSTEM

A representation of the Industrial Business Planning System is shown in Figure 10.1. The Facility Planning System is shown in the heavier lined boxes. Five planning stages can be identified.

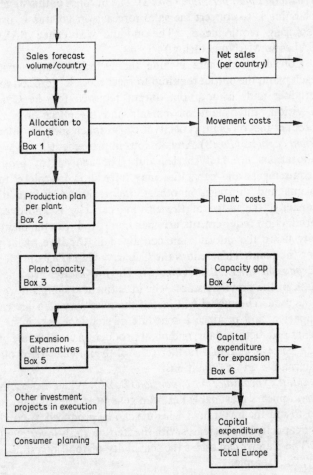

FIGURE 10.1. CPC Europe – industrial business planning system (including facilities planning).

1 *Allocation to plants* (*Box* 1). The process whereby the sales volumes of products forecasted by the Industrial Division are allocated to plants in Europe is the keystone of the planning process. From this follows the need for investment. The process of allocation to plants and the process of making an investment plan are, of course, interconnected, and recycling facilities are provided so that reallocation can take place, if this is necessary later in the cycle.

2 *Production plan per plant* (*Box* 2). The purpose of this stage of the planning is to convert the sales forecasts in volume into manufacturing requirements. (The module was called SALMAN, SALes to MANufacturing.)

Considerations here include the technical characteristics of each plant, the output required to meet the sales forecast for each product and, in addition, output required for the Consumer Division. Inter-plant movements and the effect of a varying product-mix on plant capacity are also taken into consideration.

3 *Plant capacity* (*Box* 3). Any obvious improvements to the original allocations are first carried out. The analysis of production requirements and capacities may have shown surpluses in some plants and shortages in others. Before investing in additional capacity, the usage of the existing capacity is improved. The production requirements are then compared with the plant capacity using the information contained in the investment profile for the plant. This defines the Capacity Gap (*Box* 4).

4 *Expansion alternatives* (*Box* 5). Having established the basic data in the previous stages, the investment system is now set up and used. The model will install the necessary step increases in capacity, and produce a schedule of step increases in capacity, plant production plans, and plant production costs. These outputs can be reviewed, and further runs of the model carried out with alternative set-up conditions.

5 *Capital expenditure for expansion* (*Box* 6). When a capacity plan that appears reasonable has been generated, the total investment costs and the investment schedule can be produced by combining the capacity step increases with the step quarterly investment data.

The planner can assess the sensitivity of total investment cost, by, for example,

Rerunning the system with alternative set-up conditions

Modifying the original allocation, or market plan, but using the same set-up conditions for each run.

In summary the system provides the planner with the following facilities:

(a) A calculation and display of the product sales requirements in each plant
(b) A calculation and display of the production requirements in each plant
(c) A comparison of the production requirements and the existing capacities of each production unit in each plant
(d) A method for generating a production plan and a plan for step increases in capacity for each unit in each plant
(e) A calculation of the investment requirements by unit, plant and area.

The management requirements of the system are simple to state. Underlying the computer programmes that fulfilled these requirements was an extensive analysis of the original logic used by planners, and the creation of an improved logic. The system is complex, but as an example, one part of it will be described in more detail here.

PLANT AND AREA CAPACITY INCREASE OPTIONS

It will be remember that the planning process involves running the system to install capacity steps, if demand exceeds available capacity. A number of plants in which capacity could be increased are available, so the system provides the planner with the ability to increase capacity in a particular plant to meet the demand on that plant, as originally allocated. Alternatively, he can treat plants as an area and increase capacity on that basis.

In the latter case an area is defined as a set of plants. The consolidated production requirements and capacities across these plants are compared. Where a shortage exists, any available step increase in any plant can be used to meet the requirement. The model searches for the cheapest combination of steps which will meet the shortage, subject to any time constraints imposed.

Given a set of production requirements and capacities, the step increases resulting from treating plants singly or in groups differ. The difference in investment costs show the penalty to be paid for adherence to the original allocations.

The search routine to find the cheapest combination of steps has to handle up to eight plants, with up to ten production units, each unit having a number of capacity step increases, all over a time period consisting of thirty-two quarters. It is the combination of algorithmic solutions to this type of planning situation, with the ability of the planner to incorporate his judgment, that gives the system its power.

Some idea of the flexibility and scope of the planning system can be obtained from a consideration of the following factors manipulated by the planner during his search for investment alternatives.

1 *Area for planning.* In his search for the cheapest way to plan for the additional production capacity he requires, he begins by specifying whether he wishes to consider a single plant or several plants as an area. He can, for instance, specify the single U.K. plant at Manchester, or treat the German, Dutch and French plants as one, or look at Europe as a whole. He can have capacity increases output in several ways, from which he has to choose.
2 *Production channels.* He can also select the production channels to be manipulated during the planning run.
3 *Time base, stock period, volume limits.* The plant profile part of the system contains for each plant, for each increase in capacity, the lead time necessary for installing the increase. There are thirty-two quarters in the planning period, and the user can specify a time base to be used in the planning. The actual start-up quarter is defined as the time base plus the lead time.

The stock period is the number of quarters, previous to the quarter being analysed where adjustments can be made in production levels, to cater for shortages in the quarter being analysed. In other words, the planner has the option of stockpiling during a variable earlier period.

Similarly, he can specify a volume limit, in percentage terms, by which capacity can fall short of requirements without triggering an investment step. This enables him to ignore small volume shortages. It is unreasonable, for example, to spend $500,000 to meet a capacity shortfall of 10 tons.

Under his control also he has a number of other variables associated with engineering, marketing and policy considerations.

COMPUTING FACILITIES

The programming of the system was carried out in FORTRAN. A commercial time-sharing facility whose computers were in the U.K. was used, the link being via the Belgian PTT and U.K. Post Office communications network.

USE OF THE SYSTEM

The system is in routine use in the annual planning cycle. It is used to examine a wide range of investment options, some of which are generated by the investment planners themselves, and some as a result of planning activity in the industrial, consumer or financial divisions of the organization.

Investment decisions for multi-national companies necessitate the consideration of a very wide range of factors, not all of them quantifiable. The experience and judgement of management play an important role. The Facility Planning System operates on quantifiable factors, however, and its use has given management more confidence in the accuracy of its figures when called upon to make decisions. It has made a European approach possible, in the sense that investment can be planned at a European level, as distinct from a country-by-country basis.

A maintenance programme was set up to ensure that any modifications found to be necessary as the system was used in the planning cycles were incorporated.

11. *Managing With Models*

This final chapter concentrates on the job of managing the construction and use of model-based systems. The cases dealt with in Chapters 3 to 10 were selected to illustrate some of the diverse ways in which models are being used by managers, raise some of the problems of model development and installation and list some of the technical problems that model-builders have to solve, without going into the details of techniques. The cases also underlined the principles that were set out in Chapters 1 and 2. Two of these principles are so important that we begin this chapter by repeating them, with no apology for the repetition.

THE FIRST GOLDEN RULE

The first principle concerns the attitude and orientation towards models that we believe is essential to success. We illustrate this by a sad story.

> One day we came upon a self-styled master model-builder looking sadly at the decaying ruins of his all-singing, all-dancing, seventy thousand programme-statement model. 'They won't use it', he said, and the tears rolled from downcast, misty eyes into his beard.
>
> 'It is a bit big for them, don't you think', we said. 'Why did you build it?'
>
> 'We built it', he said, and his eyes lifted as a climber's, surveying some distant Himalayan peak, 'we built it, because it wasn't there. . .'

Someone had to waste the dollars, the pounds and the marks, just to prove that it could not be done. Someone had to find out that the operational research approach to the modelling of systems, fine for optimizing the deployment of radar, fine for the solution of well-defined operational problems, was entirely unsuitable for the long-term corporate planning of Vast Unichemicals Incorporated, or even for the short-term planning of one of its brand managers.

THE EARLY DAYS

Model-builders in the early days tended to be operational researchers, management scientists, or systems analysts, and worked to produce model-based methods as an *alternative* to the way managers were running the business. They tried to model complete systems. In some cases they produced theoretically good representations of companies operating in their environments. The representations were theoretically good in that there were very many factors in their models, but practically bad in that the models became so large and complex that they were more difficult to understand than the reality that they attempted to represent. In short, the models, and the facilities that they offered, were in no way related to the needs, real and perceived, of the managers who were responsible for the business.

NOW RUN THE BUSINESS

We know of no case where a model-builder was told, 'Now run the business with your model'. That is probably just as well, for even the largest model ignores some of the quantifiable factors, and cannot handle the non-quantifiable factors at all.

This approach was, and is, wrong. Model-builders cannot build models around the way they would like to run the business (especially if they have not run any business), or even around some theoretical logic arising from the 'law of the situation'. There is not necessarily one best way. As we have stated, *ad nauseam*, and tried to show in the cases, the only way is to start from what is happening now, and to build outwards from there.

A HUMBLE BEGINNING

The model-builder's initial posture should be this: 'What I think about this situation is unimportant. What the managers, who know the situation best, think about it is very important. They are very likely to be right.' Initially the modeller must be a receiver of ideas and opinions, not a transmitter. He must have humility.

CREATIVITY AND BELONGING

Then he starts to think and to create. The process of identifying with the manager and his problems begins. As they work together, the factors change. The model-builder perhaps throws a new light on the situation. For instance, he has the time and the tools to carry out a rigorous analysis of the data, and may find something that will modify the manager's mental models. He may devise a better planning logic, a better forecasting method, a better way of handling uncertainty, and so on; better from the manager's point of view. He incorporates these in the model, but his focus of attention remains the process, not the model. His task is to devise 'decision support systems' for use *within* existing processes, perhaps to extend or modify these processes – to design tools for the managers to use, not to set up a new way of life for everyone. And he must build 'with' not 'for'. Even if he starts as an outsider, he must soon become an insider.

ADEQUATE AND PRACTICAL

Instead of attempting to model complete systems, he models those parts of the systems and the management processes that are relevant to the tasks that have to be performed, and at as high a level as possible. He does not model comprehensively: he models adequately and practically.

This lesson has yet to be learned by some organizations. We still hear of massive model-building exercises, the creation of vast useless structures, complete with incomprehensible operating manuals.

THE SECOND GOLDEN RULE – THE MODULAR APPROACH

This brings us to the second principle: our insistence on the modular approach, a phased development, carried out at the pace of the user.

In many of these cases described, this approach has been emphasized. One of the keys to success is something simple as a first step, constructed in a matter of weeks, and an effective tool used eagerly, perhaps with pride, by a manager who has played a major part in its design. A first step such as this is a sure one. The infant soon begins to walk and, with luck, falls down not at all. Most infants benefit from holding the hand of someone who has learned to walk before. So it is with models, and the system-development programme sets out the path to be taken.

THE PIT OF SIZE

The pit of size is one into which several corporations have fallen with a resounding thud. Take the case of corporate models. Realizing the errors that apartheid of modellers and users led to, some organizations tried to close the gap by insisting that the existing corporate planning processes be identified and used as the basis for a corporate model. This was a sound principle on the face of it, but one that fell down in practice for the following reasons:

1 Even when they had constructed separate models for separate areas, such as marketing, production, finance and personnel, the modellers then attempted to integrate the separate parts into a whole. The result was another inflexible giant, impossible to update and difficult to use
2 Planning procedures bring to light many decision-making processes, which cannot always be defined
3 Managers cannot always say how they do things, and they sometimes refuse to, even if they do know
4 The modellers, who were again not regarded as a real part of the management team, tried to put *all* the planning procedures and decision-making processes into one large model.

AN ENGINEERING ANALOGY

To use an engineering analogy, the managers in a business are like the operators in a jobbing shop, each a skilled craftsman running his own machine, and not like the operators tending a production line. Modellers who try to build a production line for producing plans will fail. Step by step is the rule. The first steps should be little ones, and the management machines should be kept separate.

THE TWO MANAGEMENT TASKS

There are two interacting management tasks that someone has to perform so that models may contribute effectively to running a business. The first is the management of the design and development of the systems. The second is their implementation – bringing them into use, maintaining them, and developing them as required. The first is by nature a project-planning and control task; the second is more akin to the maintenance of a manufacturing facility.

MANAGEMENT AND DESIGN DEVELOPMENT

Design and development of a model-based system should not even be started unless there is a satisfactory answer to the question, 'Why are we doing it?' An organization should never drift into the use of any management method or technique (or indeed anything else). The reasons for the exercise should be thought through. There are very many good reasons for the use of models, a number of which have emerged from the cases described, but the overriding reason for the decision to go ahead is the need for something to cope with the increasing rates of change in practically everything, and increasing uncertainty about the future.

Management is rapidly becoming more highly trained, more professional. It is not difficult for organizations to develop or buy management skills and experience. When all the competing management teams are skilled and experienced, it is the best-equipped teams that start with an advantage.

A management gladiator in the competitive marketing arena, armed only with the sword of his sharp intellect, is at a disadvantage when confronted with the machine-gun of his enemy's model-based decision-support system. One marketing manager, anxious to develop such a system for his operation, actually said to his managing director, 'Sir, you cannot send me naked into the market-place', thus echoing a British Foreign Secretary, who when advocating the continuing development of nuclear weapons, did not wish to be sent 'naked into the conference chamber'.

LEVELS OF DECISION

There are several levels at which decisions concerning development have to be made. The first is at the level of policy, where statements such as the following are made: 'It is our policy to keep abreast of management technology, and to this end we will spend $x\%$ of our profit on the development and maintenance of our systems of management.' One international company considers that it reaps two major advantages from such a policy. First, it keeps up with the work in management technology research and development agencies, such as consultants and business schools. Secondly, it believes that its managers like to work for, and are less likely to leave, a company applying 'modern' management methods. This, they believe, applies particularly to their younger managers, from whose ranks will arise their general managers of the future.

The second decision level occurs as part of the system planning task, discussed in Chapter 2. At this level the general policy 'to keep abreast of management technology' finds its first tangible manifestation. The development of models must take its rightful place in the development of the machinery of management – with the applications of Organization Development, Management by Objectives, Value Analysis programmes, cost reduction systems, the new physical distribution system, and so on.

The third level is that of programming and controlling the work. A network or bar chart representation of the project is useful and enables progress to be controlled on the seven steps discussed in Chapter 1. The programme should cover all aspects of the work, including management training courses, staff induction procedures, demonstrations of systems to interested parties, and so on. As in all control systems, the programme provides the standard with which measured progress is compared.

THE USE PHASE

The use phase begins where the development phase ends. The development programme will have considered how the systems are to be brought into use at the appropriate point in the planning cycle of the organization. The first task is to ensure that this happens, and that the inevitable user difficulties are dealt with quickly and effectively as they arise. The early days are critical, and people's attitudes to the system to a great extent depend on their first impressions. If they have been drawn into the system, the move from development to use will be smooth.

The effectiveness of the system in assisting managers to carry out their tasks should be carefully monitored during the early days of use. All suggestions and complaints should be carefully noted and recorded for subsequent action. If the system is modular, minor alterations can be carried out quickly. As in a factory, minor adjustments can be made to the machinery on a day-to-day basis, but modifications may need to be applied in a formal programme. A maintenance period for overhaul can often be fitted into the planning cycle at slack periods. It is a mistake to attempt to make major changes to model-based systems when they are in intensive use by the managers.

THE FUTURE OF MODELS

Some guidance about the development of modelling methods in the next decade can perhaps be gained by looking at what has happened in the last one. From 1965 to 1975 the rate of development has been far in excess of what most managers would have predicted in 1965. There are three main reasons for this.

Firstly, the development of electronic and computing technology has led to the production of cheaper calculating and storage devices, from the pocket calculator to the very large computer, with many users connected at the same time. The computing industry, both the hardware and the software sides, has produced computing systems with facilities that exceed management's abilities to make effective use of them. This seems likely to continue, with the production of even cheaper, smaller, and yet more powerful computing hardware, and parallel developments in software.

Secondly, the ability to construct large data bases now exists, as do methods of handling the data they contain, and that makes it easier to obtain and manipulate the data that model-based management systems require.

Thirdly, management need for manipulation of plans is much greater, because of the greater uncertainty and complexity it faces.

Had we set out to say in 1965 what was to take place in this field in the next ten years, we should not have predicted that we would be in a position to write a book on the subject, based on some 200 assorted business models constructed and in use. Nor should we have imagined ourselves using a computer in the United States from a terminal in our London offices to produce an updated market forecast on a client's terminal in Germany, or that steelmakers in Sheffield and Glasgow would be using computer terminals from their melting shops to make alloy-addition calculations on a model in a computer in London.

We hesitate, therefore, to predict for 1985, at least in any detail. We leave that to the modern soothsayers, the futurologists. However, there can be little doubt that model-based management systems are here to stay, despite the costly errors that have been made in the last ten years. We suggest this is one branch of management technology that cannot be ignored. The industrial scene is littered with the wrecks of companies that failed because they ignored changes in production technology, or could not see them coming. We believe that a number of more recent failures are due to the use of outdated management technology, in part at least. The management machinery was just not up to the strains imposed on it.

The approach suggested in this book is not costly, but the pay-off can be rapid. There seems to be no reason for delay. The technology is available, the experience has been acquired, the need is great and increasing.

We hope that we have now said enough to convince the reader that the title of this book was not chosen lightly, and that models are indeed practical and can be used effectively by managers to help with running their business. That is where we came in!

Acknowledgments

We wish to thank the Directors of The Whitehead Consulting Group for their help and encouragement during the preparation of this book. We wish also to thank the Whitehead consultants with whom we have worked over the years for the many contributions they have made to the methods and approaches described. Finally, we acknowledge our indebtedness to the many managers in industry with whom the models were built.